TRAVELING LIGHT

*Releasing the Burdens
You Were Never Intended to Bear*

Max Lucado

THOMAS NELSON
Since 1798

NASHVILLE DALLAS MEXICO CITY RIO DE JANEIRO BEIJING

Traveling Light

© 2001 Max Lucado.

Published in Nashville, Tennessee, by Thomas Nelson. Thomas Nelson is a registered trademark of Thomas Nelson, Inc.

Thomas Nelson, Inc., titles may be purchased in bulk for educational, business, fund-raising, or sales promotional use. For information, please e-mail SpecialMarkets@ThomasNelson.com.

Unless otherwise noted, Scripture quotations used in this book are from the Holy Bible, New Century Version, © 1987, 1988, 1991 by W Publishing Group, a Division of Thomas Neson, Inc., P.O. Box 141000, Nashville, Tennessee, 37214. Used by permission. Other Scripture references are from the following sources: The Holy Bible, New International Version (NIV). © 1973, 1978, 1984, International Bible Society. Used by permission of Zondervan Bible Publishers. The King James Version of the Bible (KJV). The Living Bible (TLB), © 1971 by Tyndale House Publishers, Wheaton, Ill. Used by permission. The Message (MSG), © 1993. Used by permission of NavPress Publishing Group. The New King James Version (NKJV), © 1979, 1980, 1982, Thomas Nelson, Inc., Publisher. J. B. Phillips: The New Testament in Modern English, Revised Edition (PHILLIPS). © J. B. Phillips 1958, 1960, 1972. Used by permission of Macmillan Publishing Co., Inc. The New American Standard Bible (NASB), © 1960, 1977 by the Lockman Foundation. The New Revised Standard Version Bible (NRSV), © 1989 by the Division of Christian Education of the National Council of the Churches of Christ in the USA. The Good News Bible: The Bible in Today's English Version (TEV) © 1976 by the American Bible Society. The Contemporary English Version (CEV) © 1991 by the American Bible Society. Used by permission. The New English Bible (NEB) © 1961, 1970 by the Delegates of the Oxford University Press and the Syndics of the Cambridge University Press. The Jerusalem Bible (JB) © 1966, 1967, 1968 by Darton, Longman & Todd, Ltd. and Doubleday. The Holy Bible, New Living Translation (NLT), © 1996. Used by permission of Tyndale House Publishers, Inc., Wheaton, Illinois 60189. All rights reserved.

ISBN 978-1-4002-9576-0 (SE)

Library of Congress Cataloging-in-Publication Data

Lucado, Max.
    Traveling light / by Max Lucado.
      p. cm.
    Includes bibliographical references.
    ISBN 978-0-8499-1345-7 (tp)
    ISBN 978-0-8499-1297-9 (hc)
     1. Christian life—Meditations. I. Title.

BV4501.3 .L86 2001
242—dc21

                           2001026267

Printed in the United States of America

09 10 11 12 13 BTY 5

To my dear friend Joey Paul,
celebrating thirty years of words at Word,
sharing the Word

Contents

Acknowledgments

H ere are well-deserved pats on some sturdy backs:

To Liz Heaney and Karen Hill—my editors and my assistant, midwives of the manuscript. Sorry I groaned so much.

To Steve and Cheryl Green—my representative and my friends. Because of you, contracts are read, and bills are paid, and this old boy sleeps well at night.

To Greg Pruett—Bible translator and Hebrew student. Thanks for the great insights.

To Eugene Peterson—Bible translator, author, and hero to many. Thanks for letting me use the title. And, much more, thanks for sharing your heart.

To Steve Halliday—study guide author par excellence.

To my friends at Thomas Nelson. Once again, you're the best.

To Laura Kendall and Carol Bartley—the great sleuths of the English language. Thanks for making me look smart.

To Jenna, Andrea, and Sara—my delightful daughters. I couldn't be prouder.

To Denalyn—my wife of two decades. Before you were born, where did poets go for inspiration?

To you—the reader. May the real Author speak to you.

And, most of all, to you, Jesus. The only reason we can release a burden is because you are there to take it. All the applause is yours.

The Luggage of Life

I 've never been one to travel light.

I've tried. Believe me, I've tried. But ever since I stuck three fingers in the air and took the Boy Scout pledge to be prepared, I've been determined to be exactly that—prepared.

Prepared for a bar mitzvah, baby dedication, or costume party. Prepared to parachute behind enemy lines or enter a cricket tournament. And if, perchance, the Dalai Lama might be on my flight and invite me to dine in Tibet, I carry snowshoes. One has to be prepared.

I don't know how to travel light.

Fact is, there's a lot about travel I don't know. I don't know how to interpret the restrictions of a supersaver seat—*half price if you leave on Wednesdays during duck-hunting season and return when the moon is full in a nonelection year.* I don't know why they don't build the whole plane out of the same metal they use to build the little black box. I don't know how to escape the airplane toilet without sacrificing one of my extremities to the jaws of the folding door. And I don't know what to say to guys like the taxi driver in Rio who learned I was an American and asked me if I knew his cousin Eddie who lives in the U.S.

There's a lot about traveling I don't know.

I don't know why we men would rather floss a crocodile than ask for directions. I don't know why vacation slides aren't used to treat insomnia, and I don't know when I'll learn not to eat food whose names I can't pronounce.

But most of all, I don't know how to travel light.

I don't know how to travel without granola bars, sodas, and rain gear. I don't know how to travel without flashlights and a generator and a global tracking system. I don't know how to travel without an ice chest of wieners. What if I stumble upon a backyard barbecue? To bring nothing to the party would be rude.

Every travel-catalog company in the world has my credit-card number. I've got an iron that doubles as a paperweight, a hair dryer the size of a coach's whistle, a Swiss Army knife that expands into a pup tent, and a pair of pants that inflate upon impact. (On one flight my wife, Denalyn, gave me a swat on the leg, and I couldn't get out of my seat.)

I don't know how to travel light. But I need to learn. Denalyn refuses to give birth to any more children even though the airlines allow each passenger three checked bags and two carry-ons.

I need to learn to travel light.

You're wondering why I can't. *Loosen up!* you're thinking. *You can't enjoy a journey carrying so much stuff. Why don't you just drop all that luggage?*

Funny you should ask. I'd like to inquire the same of you. Haven't you been known to pick up a few bags?

Odds are, you did this morning. Somewhere between the first step on the floor and the last step out the door, you grabbed some luggage. You stepped over to the baggage carousel and loaded up. Don't remember doing so? That's because you did it without thinking. Don't remember seeing a baggage terminal? That's because the carousel is not the one in the airport; it's the one in the mind. And the bags we grab are not made of leather; they're made of burdens.

The suitcase of guilt. A sack of discontent. You drape a duffel bag of weariness on one shoulder and a hanging bag of grief on the other. Add on a backpack of doubt, an overnight bag of loneliness, and a trunk of fear. Pretty soon you're pulling more stuff than a skycap. No wonder you're so tired at the end of the day. Lugging luggage is exhausting.

What you were saying to me, God is saying to you, "Set that stuff down! You're carrying burdens you don't need to bear."

"Come to me," he invites, "all of you who are weary and carry heavy burdens, and I will give you rest" (Matt. 11:28 NLT).

If we let him, God will lighten our loads . . . but how do we let him? May I invite an old friend to show us? The Twenty-third Psalm.

> The LORD is my shepherd;
> I shall not want.
> He makes me to lie down in green pastures;
> He leads me beside the still waters.
> He restores my soul;
> He leads me in the paths of righteousness
> For His name's sake.
>
> Yea, though I walk through the valley of the shadow of death,
> I will fear no evil;
> For You are with me;
> Your rod and Your staff, they comfort me.
>
> You prepare a table before me in the presence of my enemies;
> You anoint my head with oil.
> My cup runs over.
> Surely goodness and mercy shall follow me
> All the days of my life;
> And I will dwell in the house of the LORD
> Forever. (NKJV)

Do more beloved words exist? Framed and hung in hospital halls, scratched on prison walls, quoted by the young, and whispered by the dying. In these lines sailors have found a harbor, the frightened have found a father, and strugglers have found a friend.

And because the passage is so deeply loved, it is widely known. Can you find ears on which these words have never fallen? Set to music in a hundred songs, translated into a thousand tongues, domiciled in a million hearts.

One of those hearts might be yours. What kinship do you feel with these words? Where do the verses transport you? To a fireside? Bedside? Graveside?

Hardly a week passes that I don't turn to them. This passage is to the minister what balm is to the physician. I recently applied them to the heart of a dear friend. Summoned to his house with the words "The doctors aren't giving him more than a few days," I looked at him and understood. Face pale. Lips stretched and parched. Skin draping between bones like old umbrella cloth between spokes. The cancer had taken so much: his appetite, his strength, his days. But the cancer hadn't touched his faith. Pulling a chair to his bed and squeezing his hand, I whispered, "Bill, 'The Lord is my shepherd; I shall not want.'" He rolled his head toward me as if to welcome the words.

"He makes me to lie down in green pastures; He leads me beside the still waters. He restores my soul; He leads me in the paths of righteousness for His name's sake."

Reaching the fourth verse, fearful that he might not hear, I leaned forward until I was a couple of inches from his ear and said, "Though I walk through the valley of the shadow of death, I will fear no evil; for You are with me; Your rod and Your staff, they comfort me."

He didn't open his eyes, but he arched his brows. He didn't speak, but his thin fingers curled around mine, and I wondered if the Lord was helping him set down some luggage, the fear of dying.

Do you have some luggage of your own? Do you think God might use David's psalm to lighten your load? *Traveling light means trusting God with the burdens you were never intended to bear.*

Why don't you try traveling light? Try it for the sake of those you love. Have you ever considered the impact that excess baggage has on relationships? We've made this point at our church by virtue of a drama. A wedding is reenacted in which we hear the thoughts of the bride and groom. The groom enters, laden with luggage. A bag dangles from every appendage. And each bag is labeled: guilt, anger, arrogance, insecurities. This fellow is loaded. As he stands at the altar, the audience hears him thinking, *Finally, a woman who will help me carry all my burdens. She's so strong, so stable, so . . .*

As his thoughts continue, hers begin. She enters, wearing a wedding gown but, like her fiancé, covered with luggage. Pulling a hanging bag, shouldering a carry-on, hauling a makeup kit, paper sack—everything you could imagine and everything labeled. She has her own bags: prejudice, loneliness, disappointments. And her expectations? Listen to what she is thinking: *Just a few more minutes and I've got me a man. No more counselors. No more group sessions. So long, discouragement and worry. I won't be seeing you anymore. He's going to fix me.*

Finally they stand at the altar, lost in a mountain of luggage. They smile their way through the ceremony, but when given the invitation to kiss each other, they can't. How do you embrace someone if your arms are full of bags?

For the sake of those you love, learn to set them down.

And, for the sake of the God you serve, do the same. He wants to use you, you know. But how can he if you are exhausted? This truth came home to me yesterday afternoon on a run. Preparing for a jog, I couldn't decide what to wear. The sun was out, but the wind was chilly. The sky was clear, but the forecast said rain. Jacket or sweatshirt? The Boy Scout within me prevailed. I wore both.

I grabbed my Walkman but couldn't decide which tape to bring. A sermon or music? You guessed it, I took both. Needing to stay in touch with my kids, I carried a cell phone. So no one would steal my car, I pocketed my keys. As a precaution against thirst, I brought along some drink money in a pouch. I looked more like a pack mule than a runner! Within half a mile I was peeling off the jacket and hiding it in a bush. That kind of weight will slow you down.

What's true in jogging is true in faith. God has a great race for you to run. Under his care you will go where you've never been and serve in ways you've never dreamed. But you have to drop some stuff. How can you share grace if you are full of guilt? How can you offer comfort if you are disheartened? How can you lift someone else's load if your arms are full with your own?

For the sake of those you love, travel light.

For the sake of the God you serve, travel light.

For the sake of your own joy, travel light.

There are certain weights in life you simply cannot carry. Your Lord is asking you to set them down and trust him. He is the father at the baggage claim. When a dad sees his five-year-old son trying to drag the family trunk off the carousel, what does he say? The father will say to his son what God is saying to you,

"Set it down, child. I'll carry that one."

What do you say we take God up on his offer? We just might find ourselves traveling a little lighter.

By the way, I may have overstated my packing problems. (I don't usually take snowshoes.) But I can't overstate God's promise: "Unload all your worries onto him, since he is looking after you" (1 Pet. 5:7 JB).

2

The Middle C of Life

The Burden of a Lesser God

The LORD . . .

I 'm only five feet from an eagle. His wings are spread, and his talons are lifted above the branch. White feathers cap his head, and black eyes peer at me from both sides of a golden beak. He is so close I could touch him. So near I could stroke him. With only a lean and a stretch of my right arm, I could cover the eagle's crown with my hand.

But I don't. I don't reach. Why not? Am I afraid of him?

Hardly. He hasn't budged in two years. When I first opened the box, he impressed me. When I first set him on the shelf, I admired him. Man-made eagles are nice for a while, but you quickly get used to them.

David is concerned that you and I don't make the same mistake with God. His pen has scarcely touched papyrus, and he's urging us to avoid gods of our own making. With his very first words in this psalm, David sets out to deliver us from the burden of a lesser deity.

One might argue that he seeks to do nothing else. For though he will speak of green pastures, his thesis is not rest. He will describe death's somber valley, but this poem is not an ode to dying. He will tell of the Lord's forever house, but his theme is not heaven. Why did David write the Twenty-third Psalm? To build our trust in God . . . to remind us of who he is.

In this psalm David devotes one hundred and fifteen words to explaining the first two:[1] "The LORD." In the arena of unnecessary luggage, the psalmist begins with the weightiest: the refashioned god. One who looks nice but does little. God as . . .

A genie in a bottle. Convenient. Congenial. Need a parking place, date, field goal made or missed? All you do is rub the bottle and *poof*—it's yours. And, what's even better, this god goes back into the bottle after he's done.

A sweet grandpa. So soft hearted. So wise. So kind. But very, very, very old. Grandpas are great when they are awake, but they tend to doze off when you need them.

A busy dad. Leaves on Mondays, returns on Saturdays. Lots of road trips and business meetings. He'll show up on Sunday, however, so clean up and look spiritual. On Monday, be yourself again. He'll never know.

Ever held these views of God? If so, you know the problems they cause. A busy dad doesn't have time for your questions. A kind grandpa is too weak to carry your load. And if your god is a genie in a bottle, then you are greater than he is. He comes and goes at your command.

A god who looks nice but does little.

Reminds me of a briefcase I own. Though I'd like to fault the salesman, I can't. The purchase was my decision. But he certainly made it easy. I didn't need a new satchel. The one I had was fine. Scarred and scratched but fine. The paint was worn off the zippers, and the edges were scuffed, but the bag was fine.

Oh, but this new one, to use the words of the college-age boy in the leather store, was "really fine." Loaded with features: copper covers on the corners, smooth leather from Spain, and, most of all, an Italian name near the handle. The salesman gave his line and handed me the bag, and I bought them both.

I left the store with a briefcase that I have used maybe twice. What was I thinking? It carries so little. My old bag had no copper-covered corners, but it had a belly like a beluga. This new one reminds me of a high-fashion model: slim, stiff, and tight-lipped. A book and a newspaper, and this Italian satchel is *"fullisimo."*

The bag looks nice but does nothing.

Is that the kind of God you want? Is that the kind of God we have?

David's answer is a resounding no. "You want to know who God really is?" he asks. "Then read this." And he writes the name *Yahweh.* "Yahweh is my shepherd."

Though foreign to us, the name was rich to David. So rich, in fact, that David chose *Yahweh* over *El Shaddai* (God Almighty), *El Elyon* (God Most High), and *El Olam* (God the Everlasting). These and many other titles for God were at David's disposal. But when he considered all the options, David chose *Yahweh.*

Why *Yahweh?* Because *Yahweh* is God's name. You can call me preacher or writer or half-baked golfer—these are accurate descriptions, but these aren't my names. I might call you dad, mom, doctor, or student, and those terms may describe you, but they aren't your name. If you want to call me by my name, say *Max.* If I call you by your name, I say it. And if you want to call God by his name, say *Yahweh.*

God has told us his name. (How he must long to be close to us.)

Moses was the first to learn it. Seven centuries prior to David, the eighty-year-old shepherd was tending sheep when the bush began to blaze and his life began to change. Moses was told to return to Egypt and rescue the enslaved Hebrews. He raised more excuses than a kid at bedtime, but God trumped each one. Finally Moses asked,

"When I go to the Israelites, I will say to them, 'The God of your fathers sent me to you.' What if the people say, 'What is his name?' What should I tell them?"

Then God said to Moses, "I AM WHO I AM. When you go to the people of Israel, tell them, 'I AM sent me to you.'" (Exod. 3:13–14)

God would later remind Moses: "I am Yahweh. To Abraham and Isaac and Jacob I appeared as El Shaddai; I did not make myself known to them by my name Yahweh" (Exod. 6:2–3 JB).

The Israelites considered the name too holy to be spoken by human lips. Whenever they needed to say *Yahweh,* they substituted the word *Adonai,* which means "Lord." If the name needed to be written, the scribes would take a bath before they wrote it and destroy the pen afterward.[2]

God never gives a definition of the word *Yahweh,* and Moses never requests one. Many scholars wish he had, for the study of the name has raised some healthy discussions.

The name I AM sounds strikingly close to the Hebrew verb *to be—havah.* It's quite possibly a combination of the present tense form (I am) and the causative tense (I cause to be). *Yahweh,* then, seems to mean "I AM" and "I cause." God is the "One who is" and the "One who causes."

Why is that important? Because we need a big God. And if God is the "One who is," then he is an unchanging God.

Think about it. Do you know anyone who goes around saying, "I am"? Neither do I. When we say "I am," we always add another word. "I am *happy.*" "I am *sad.*" "I am *strong.*" "I am *Max.*" God, however, starkly states, "I AM" and adds nothing else.

"You are what?" we want to ask. "I AM," he replies. God needs no descriptive word because he never changes. God is what he is. He is what he has always been. His immutability motivated the psalmist to declare, "But thou art the same" (Ps. 102:27 KJV). The writer is saying, "You are the One who is. You never change."[3] Yahweh is an unchanging God.

He is also an uncaused God.

Though he creates, God was never created. Though he makes, he was never made. Though he causes, he was never caused. Hence the psalmist's proclamation: "Before the mountains were born or you brought forth the earth and the world, from everlasting to everlasting you are God" (Ps. 90:2 NIV).

God is Yahweh—an unchanging God, an uncaused God, and an ungoverned God.

You and I are governed. The weather determines what we wear. The terrain tells us how to travel. Gravity dictates our speed, and health determines our strength. We may challenge these forces and alter them slightly, but we never remove them.

God—our Shepherd—doesn't check the weather; he makes it. He doesn't defy gravity; he created it. He isn't affected by health; he has no body. Jesus said, "God is spirit" (John 4:24). Since he has no body, he has no limitations—equally active in Cambodia as he is in Connecticut. "Where can I go to get away from your Spirit?" asked David. "Where can I run from you? If I go up to the heavens, you are there. If I lie down in the grave, you are there" (Ps. 139:7–8).

Unchanging. Uncaused. Ungoverned. These are only a fraction of God's qualities, but aren't they enough to give you a glimpse of your Father? Don't we need this kind of shepherd? Don't we need an unchanging shepherd?

When Lloyd Douglas, author of The Robe and other novels, attended college, he lived in a boardinghouse. A retired, wheelchair-bound music professor resided on the first floor. Each morning Douglas would stick his head in the door of the teacher's apartment and ask the same question, "Well, what's the good news?" The old man would pick up his tuning fork, tap it on the side of the wheelchair, and say, "That's middle C! It was middle C yesterday; it will be middle C tomorrow; it will be middle C a thousand years from now. The tenor upstairs sings flat. The piano across the hall is out of tune, but, my friend, that is middle C."[4]

You and I need a middle C. Haven't you had enough change in your life? Relationships change. Health changes. The weather changes. But the Yahweh who ruled the earth last night is the same Yahweh who rules it today. Same convictions. Same plan. Same mood. Same love. He never changes. You can no more alter God than a pebble can alter the rhythm of the Pacific. Yahweh is our middle C. A still point in a turning world. Don't we need a still point? Don't we need an unchanging shepherd?

We equally need an uncaused shepherd. No one breathed life into Yahweh. No one sired him. No one gave birth to him. No one caused him. No act brought him forth.

And since no act brought him forth, no act can take him out. Does he fear an earthquake? Does he tremble at a tornado? Hardly. Yahweh sleeps through storms and calms the winds with a word. Cancer does not trouble him, and cemeteries do not disturb him. He was here before they came. He'll be here after they are gone. He is uncaused.

And he is ungoverned. Counselors can comfort you *in* the storm, but you need a God who can *still* the storm. Friends can hold your hand at your deathbed, but you need a Yahweh who has defeated the grave. Philosophers can debate the meaning of life, but you need a Lord who can declare the meaning of life.

You need a Yahweh.

You don't need what Dorothy found. Remember her discovery in *The Wonderful Wizard of Oz?* She and her trio followed the yellow-brick road only to discover that the wizard was a wimp! Nothing but smoke and mirrors and tin-drum thunder. Is that the kind of god you need?

You don't need to carry the burden of a lesser god . . . a god on a shelf, a god in a box, or a god in a bottle. No, you need a God who can place 100 billion stars in our galaxy and 100 billion galaxies in the universe. You need a God who can shape two fists of flesh into 75 to 100 billion nerve cells, each with as many as 10,000 connections to other nerve cells, place it in a skull, and call it a brain.[5]

And you need a God who, while so mind-numbingly mighty, can come in the soft of night and touch you with the tenderness of an April snow.

You need a Yahweh.

And, according to David, you have one. He is your shepherd.

I'll Do It My Way

The Burden of Self-Reliance

The LORD is my shepherd.

PSALM 23:1 NKJV

Y ou say you can swing a club like Tiger Woods? That's saying a lot.

You hope to score touchdowns like Joe Montana? You'll have to work hard.

And you, young lady? You aspire to be the next Mia Hamm? Good for you.

And me? Well, actually there is one fellow who's caught my attention. He reminds me of me. You've probably never heard of him. Did you see the British Open in '99? Yeah, the one in Carnoustie, Scotland? Remember the player who had a seven-stroke lead with one hole to go?

That's right, the Frenchman. Jean Van de Velde. He was six strokes and 480 yards away from a major championship, a wad of cash, and a place in history. All he needed to do was score a six on a par four.

I could shoot a six on a par four. My mother could make a six on a par four. This guy could shoot a six with a waffle iron and a banana. Tell the trophy engraver to warm up the pen and practice his Vs. He'll need two to write "Jean Van de Velde."

Granted the hole was not easy. Bisected three times by a "wee burn," the Scottish term for a marshy creek. No sweat. Hit three short shots . . . putt three times if you have to. Just take a six, win the hole, and smile for the cameras. Besides it's windy, and the "wee burn" is wee deep. Don't flirt with it.

Oh, but the French love to flirt. Van de Velde pulls out his driver, and somewhere in Des Moines an armchair duffer who'd been lured to sleep by the seven-stroke lead opens one eye. *He's holding a driver?*

Van de Velde's caddie was a thirty-year-old Parisian named Christopher with untidy English and a paintbrush on his chin and bleached hair under his hat. "I think he and I—we want too much show," he later confessed.

Van de Velde pushes his drive halfway to the Eiffel Tower. Now he has 240 yards to the green with nothing but deep grass and heartache in between. Surely he will hit a short shot back in the fairway.

Logic says, "Don't go for the green."

Golf 101 says, "Don't go for the green."

Every Scot in the gallery says, "Aye, laddie. Don't go for the green."

Van de Velde says, "I'm going for the green."

He pulls out a two iron, and the armchair golfer in Des Moines opens the other eye. *A two iron!? Maybe if you're teed up on the beach, trying to hit into the Caribbean!* The spectators are silent. Most out of respect. A few in prayer. Van de Velde's two iron becomes a FORE! iron. *Whack. Clang. Plop.* The ball caroms off the bleachers and disappears into marsh tall enough to hide a lawn gnome.

His lie would've made Pinocchio's nose grow. The next shot lands in the water and the next in the sand. Tally the damage, and you've got four strokes plus a penalty. He's lying five and not on the green. So much for winning the hole. By now he's praying for a seven and a tie. To the great relief of the civilized world, Van de Velde makes the seven. You've got to wonder if he ever recovered from the "wee burn." He lost the play-off.

Golf, like nylon running shorts, reveals a lot about a person. What the eighteenth hole revealed about Van de Velde reminds me of me.

I've done the same thing. The same blasted thing. All he needed was a five iron, but he had to go and pull out the driver. Or, in my case:

All I needed to do was apologize, but I had to argue.

All I needed to do was listen, but I had to open my big mouth.

All I needed to do was be patient, but I had to take control.

All I had to do was give it to God, but I tried to fix it myself.

Why don't I leave the driver in the bag? I know how Christopher the caddie would answer: "I think he and I and Max—we want too much show."

Too much stubbornness. Too much independence. Too much self-reliance.

I don't need advice—*Whack*.

I can handle this myself—*Clang*.

I don't need a shepherd, thank you—*Plop*.

Can you relate? Are Jean and I the only ones to make an anthem out of Sinatra's song "I Did It My Way"? Are we the only two dragging around the cast-iron chest of self-reliance? I don't think so.

We humans want to do things our way. Forget the easy way. Forget the common way. Forget the best way. Forget God's way. We want to do things *our* way.

And, according to the Bible, that's precisely our problem. "We all have wandered away like sheep; each of us has gone his own way" (Isa. 53:6).

You wouldn't think sheep would be obstinate. Of all God's animals, the sheep is the least able to take care of himself.

Sheep are dumb! Have you ever met a sheep trainer? Ever seen sheep tricks? Know anyone who has taught his sheep to roll over? Ever witnessed a circus sideshow featuring "Mazadon and his jumping sheep"? No. Sheep are just too dumb.

And defenseless. They have no fangs or claws. They can't bite you or outrun you. That's why you never see sheep as team mascots. We've heard of the St. Louis Rams and the Chicago Bulls and the Seattle

Seahawks, but the New York Lambs? Who wants to be a lamb? You couldn't even stir up a decent yell for the cheerleaders.

> We are the sheep.
> We don't make a peep.
> Victory is yours to keep.
> But count us if you want to sleep.

What's more, sheep are dirty. A cat can clean itself. So can a dog. We see a bird in a birdbath or a bear in a river. But sheep? They get dirty and stay that way.

Couldn't David have thought of a better metaphor? Surely he could have. After all, he outran Saul and outgunned Goliath. Why didn't he choose something other than sheep?

How about:

"The Lord is my commander in chief, and I am his warrior." There. We like that better. A warrior gets a uniform and a weapon, maybe even a medal.

Or, "The Lord is my inspiration, and I am his singer." We are in God's choir; what a flattering assignment.

Or, "The Lord is my king, and I am his ambassador." Who wouldn't like to be a spokesperson for God?

Everyone stops when the ambassador speaks. Everyone listens when God's minstrel sings. Everyone applauds when God's warrior passes.

But who notices when God's sheep show up? Who notices when the sheep sing or speak or act? Only one person notices. The shepherd. And that is precisely David's point.

When David, who was a warrior, minstrel, and ambassador for God, searched for an illustration of God, he remembered his days as a shepherd. He remembered how he lavished attention on the sheep day and night. How he slept with them and watched over them.

And the way he cared for the sheep reminded him of the way God cares for us. David rejoiced to say, "The LORD is my shepherd," and in so doing he proudly implied, "I am his sheep."

Still uncomfortable with being considered a sheep? Will you humor me and take a simple quiz? See if you succeed in self-reliance. Raise your hand if any of the following describe you.

You can control your moods. You're never grumpy or sullen. You can't relate to Jekyll and Hyde. You're always upbeat and upright. Does that describe you? No? Well, let's try another.

You are at peace with everyone. Every relationship as sweet as fudge. Even your old flames speak highly of you. Love all and are loved by all. Is that you? If not, how about this description?

You have no fears. Call you the Teflon toughie. Wall Street plummets—no problem. Heart condition discovered—yawn. World War III starts—what's for dinner? Does this describe you?

You need no forgiveness. Never made a mistake. As square as a game of checkers. As clean as grandma's kitchen. Never cheated, never lied, never lied about cheating. Is that you? No?

Let's evaluate this. You can't control your moods. A few of your relationships are shaky. You have fears and faults. Hmmm. Do you really want to hang on to your chest of self-reliance? Sounds to me as if you could use a shepherd. Otherwise, you might end up with a Twenty-third Psalm like this:

I am my own shepherd. I am always in need.

I stumble from mall to mall and shrink to shrink, seeking relief but never finding it.

I creep through the valley of the shadow of death and fall apart.

I fear everything from pesticides to power lines, and I'm starting to act
like my mother.

I go down to the weekly staff meeting and am surrounded by enemies.

I go home, and even my goldfish scowls at me.

I anoint my headache with extra-strength Tylenol.

My Jack Daniel's runneth over.

Surely misery and misfortune will follow me, and I will live in self-
doubt for the rest of my lonely life.

Why is it that the ones who most need a shepherd resist him so?

Ah, now there is a question for the Van de Veldes of life. Scripture
says, "Do it God's way." Experience says, "Do it God's way." Every Scot
in heaven begs, "Aye, laddie, do it God's way."

And, every so often, we do. And when we do, when we follow the
lead of *Notre Dieu* and keep the driver in the bag, somehow the ball
stays in the fairway.

Yes, Van de Velde reminds me of me.

After losing the play-off hole, he kept his composure for the crowds.
But once he sat in the scorer's tent, he buried his face in his hands. "Next
time I'll hit zee wedge," he sobbed. "You'll say I'm a coward, but next
time I'll hit zee wedge."

You and me both, Jean.[1]

The Prison of Want

The Burden of Discontent

The LORD is my shepherd; I shall not want.

PSALM 23:1 NKJV

C ome with me to the most populated prison in the world. The facility has more inmates than bunks. More prisoners than plates. More residents than resources.

Come with me to the world's most oppressive prison. Just ask the inmates; they will tell you. They are overworked and underfed. Their walls are bare and bunks are hard.

No prison is so populated, no prison so oppressive, and, what's more, no prison is so permanent. Most inmates never leave. They never escape. They never get released. They serve a life sentence in this overcrowded, underprovisioned facility.

The name of the prison? You'll see it over the entrance. Rainbowed over the gate are four cast-iron letters that spell out its name:

W-A-N-T

The prison of want. You've seen her prisoners. They are "in want." They want something. They want something bigger. Nicer. Faster. Thinner. They want.

They don't want much, mind you. They want just one thing. One new job. One new car. One new house. One new spouse. They don't want much. They want just one.

And when they have "one," they will be happy. And they are right—

they will be happy. When they have "one," they will leave the prison. But then it happens. The new-car smell passes. The new job gets old. The neighbors buy a larger television set. The new spouse has bad habits. The sizzle fizzles, and before you know it, another ex-con breaks parole and returns to jail.

Are you in prison? You are if you feel better when you have more and worse when you have less. You are if joy is one delivery away, one transfer away, one award away, or one makeover away. If your happiness comes from something you deposit, drive, drink, or digest, then face it—you are in prison, the prison of want.

That's the bad news. The good news is, you have a visitor. And your visitor has a message that can get you paroled. Make your way to the receiving room. Take your seat in the chair, and look across the table at the psalmist David. He motions for you to lean forward. "I have a secret to tell you," he whispers, "the secret of satisfaction. 'The LORD is my shepherd; I shall not want'" (Ps. 23:1 NKJV).

David has found the pasture where discontent goes to die. It's as if he is saying, "What I have in God is greater than what I don't have in life."

You think you and I could learn to say the same?

Think for just a moment about the things you own. Think about the house you have, the car you drive, the money you've saved. Think about the jewelry you've inherited and the stocks you've traded and the clothes you've purchased. Envision all your stuff, and let me remind you of two biblical truths.

Your stuff isn't yours. Ask any coroner. Ask any embalmer. Ask any funeral-home director. No one takes anything with him. When one of the wealthiest men in history, John D. Rockefeller, died, his account-ant was asked, "How much did John D. leave?" The accountant's reply? "All of it."[1]

"Naked a man comes from his mother's womb, and as he comes, so he departs. He takes nothing from his labor that he can carry in his hand" (Eccles. 5:15 NIV).

All that stuff—it's not yours. And you know what else about all that stuff? *It's not you.* Who you are has nothing to do with the clothes you wear or the car you drive. Jesus said, "Life is not defined by what you have, even when you have a lot" (Luke 12:15 MSG). Heaven does not know you as the fellow with the nice suit or the woman with the big house or the kid with the new bike. Heaven knows your heart. "The LORD does not look at the things man looks at. Man looks at the outward appearance, but the LORD looks at the heart" (1 Sam. 16:7 NIV). When God thinks of you, he may see your compassion, your devotion, your tenderness or quick mind, but he doesn't think of your things.

And when you think of you, you shouldn't either. Define yourself by your stuff, and you'll feel good when you have a lot and bad when you don't. Contentment comes when we can honestly say with Paul: "I have learned to be satisfied with the things I have. . . . I know how to live when I am poor, and I know how to live when I have plenty" (Phil. 4:11–12).

Doug McKnight could say those words. At the age of thirty-two he was diagnosed with multiple sclerosis. Over the next sixteen years it would cost him his career, his mobility, and eventually his life. Because of MS, he couldn't feed himself or walk; he battled depression and fear. But through it all, Doug never lost his sense of gratitude. Evidence of this was seen in his prayer list. Friends in his congregation asked him to compile a list of requests so they could intercede for him. His response included eighteen blessings for which to be grateful and six concerns for which to be prayerful. His blessings outweighed his needs by three times. Doug McKnight had learned to be content.[2]

So had the leper on the island of Tobago. A short-term missionary met her on a mission trip. On the final day, he was leading worship in a leper colony. He asked if anyone had a favorite song. When he did, a woman turned around, and he saw the most disfigured face he'd ever seen. She had no ears and no nose. Her lips were gone. But she raised a fingerless hand and asked, "Could we sing 'Count Your Many Blessings'?"

The missionary started the song but couldn't finish. Someone later commented, "I suppose you'll never be able to sing the song again." He answered, "No, I'll sing it again. Just never in the same way."[3]

Are you hoping that a change in circumstances will bring a change in your attitude? If so, you are in prison, and you need to learn a secret of traveling light. *What you have in your Shepherd is greater than what you don't have in life.*

May I meddle for a moment? What is the one thing separating you from joy? How do you fill in this blank: "I will be happy when _____"? When I am healed. When I am promoted. When I am married. When I am single. When I am rich. How would you finish that statement?

Now, with your answer firmly in mind, answer this. If your ship never comes in, if your dream never comes true, if the situation never changes, could you be happy? If not, then you are sleeping in the cold cell of discontent. You are in prison. And you need to know what you have in your Shepherd.

You have a God who hears you, the power of love behind you, the Holy Spirit within you, and all of heaven ahead of you. If you have the Shepherd, you have grace for every sin, direction for every turn, a candle for every corner, and an anchor for every storm. You have everything you need.

And who can take it from you? Can leukemia infect your salvation? Can bankruptcy impoverish your prayers? A tornado might take your earthly house, but will it touch your heavenly home?

And look at your position. Why clamor for prestige and power? Are you not already privileged to be part of the greatest work in history?

According to Russ Blowers, we are. He is a minister in Indianapolis. Knowing he would be asked about his profession at a Rotary Club meeting, he resolved to say more than "I'm a preacher."

Instead he explained, "Hi, I'm Russ Blowers. I'm with a global enterprise. We have branches in every country in the world. We have representatives in nearly every parliament and boardroom on earth. We're into motivation and behavior alteration. We run hospitals, feeding stations, crisis-pregnancy centers, universities, publishing houses, and nursing homes. We care for our clients from birth to death. We are into life insurance and fire insurance. We perform spiritual heart transplants. Our original Organizer owns all the real estate on earth plus an assortment of galaxies and constellations. He knows everything and lives everywhere. Our product is free for the asking. (There's not enough money to buy it.) Our CEO was born in a hick town, worked as a carpenter, didn't own a home, was misunderstood by his family and hated by his enemies, walked on water, was condemned to death without a trial, and arose from the dead. I talk with him every day."[4]

If you can say the same, don't you have reason to be content?

A man once went to a minister for counseling. He was in the midst of a financial collapse. "I've lost everything," he bemoaned.

"Oh, I'm so sorry to hear that you've lost your faith."

"No," the man corrected him, "I haven't lost my faith."

"Well, then I'm sad to hear that you've lost your character."

"I didn't say that," he corrected. "I still have my character."

"I'm so sorry to hear that you've lost your salvation."

"That's not what I said," the man objected. "I haven't lost my salvation."

"You have your faith, your character, your salvation. Seems to me," the minister observed, "that you've lost none of the things that really matter."

We haven't either. You and I could pray like the Puritan. He sat down to a meal of bread and water. He bowed his head and declared, "All this and Jesus too?"

Can't we be equally content? Paul says that "godliness with contentment is great gain" (1 Tim. 6:6 NIV). When we surrender to God the cumbersome sack of discontent, we don't just give up something; we gain something. God replaces it with a lightweight, tailor-made, sorrow-resistant attaché of gratitude.

What will you gain with contentment? You may gain your marriage. You may gain precious hours with your children. You may gain your self-respect. You may gain joy. You may gain the faith to say, "The LORD is my shepherd; I shall not want."

Try saying it slowly. "The LORD is my shepherd; I shall not want."

Again, "The LORD is my shepherd; I shall not want."

Again, "The LORD is my shepherd; I shall not want."

Shhhhhhh. Did you hear something? I think I did. I'm not sure . . . but I think I heard the opening of a jail door.

5

I Will Give You Rest

The Burden of Weariness

He makes me to lie down in green pastures.

PSALM 23:2 NKJV

 'll give you the consequences of the burden; you guess the cause.

- It afflicts 70 million Americans and is faulted for 38,000 deaths each year.

- The condition annually costs the U.S. $70 billion worth of productivity.

- Teenagers suffer from it. Studies show that 64 percent of teens blame it for poor school performance.

- Middle agers face it. Researchers say the most severe cases occur between ages thirty and forty.

- Senior citizens are afflicted by it. One study suggests that the condition impacts 50 percent of the over-sixty-five population.

- Treatments involve everything from mouth guards to herbal teas to medication.[1]

Any idea what's being described?

Chemical abuse? Divorce? Long sermons? None of those answers are correct, though the last one was a good hunch. The answer may surprise you. Insomnia. America can't get to sleep.

For most of my life I secretly snickered at the thought of sleep difficulties. My problem was not in going to sleep. My problem was staying awake. But a few years ago I went to bed one night, closed my eyes, and nothing happened. I didn't fall asleep. Rather than slow to a halt, my mind kicked into high gear. A thousand and one obligations rushed at me. Midnight passed, and I was still awake. I drank some milk, returned to bed. I was still awake. I woke up Denalyn, using the blue ribbon of dumb questions, "Are you awake?" She told me to quit thinking about things. So I did. I quit thinking about things and started thinking about people. But as I thought of people, I thought of what those people were doing. They were sleeping. That made me mad and kept me awake. Finally, somewhere in the early hours of the morning, having been initiated into the fraternity of 70 million sleepless Americans, I dozed off.

I don't snicker at the thought of sleep difficulties anymore. Nor do I question the inclusion of the verse about rest in the Twenty-third Psalm.

People with too much work and too little sleep step over to the baggage claim of life and grab the duffel bag of weariness. You don't carry this one. You don't hoist it onto your shoulder and stride down the street. You drag it as you would a stubborn St. Bernard. Weariness wearies.

Why are we so tired? Have you read a newspaper lately? We long to have the life of Huck and Tom on the Mississippi, but look at us riding the white waters of the Rio Grande. Forks in the river. Rocks in the water. Heart attacks, betrayal, credit-card debt, and custody battles. Huck and Tom didn't have to face these kinds of things. We do, however, and they keep us awake. And since we can't sleep, we have a second problem.

Our bodies are tired. Think about it. If 70 million Americans aren't sleeping enough, what does that mean? That means one-third of our country is dozing off at work, napping through class, or sleeping at the wheel. (Fifteen hundred road deaths per year are blamed on heavy-eyed truckdrivers.) Some even snooze while reading Lucado books.

(Hard to fathom, I know.) Thirty tons of aspirins, sleeping pills, and tranquilizers are consumed every day![2] The energy gauge on the dashboard of our forehead says empty.

Were we to invite an alien to solve our problem, he'd suggest a simple solution—everybody go to sleep. We'd laugh at him. He doesn't understand the way we work. Literally. He doesn't understand *the way* we work. We work hard. There is money to be made. Degrees to be earned. Ladders to be climbed. In our book, busyness is next to godliness. We idolize Thomas Edison, who claimed he could live on fifteen-minute naps. Somehow we forget to mention Albert Einstein, who averaged eleven hours of sleep a night.[3] In 1910 Americans slept nine hours a night; today we sleep seven and are proud of it. And we are tired because of it. Our minds are tired. Our bodies are tired. But much more important, our souls are tired.

We are eternal creatures, and we ask eternal questions: Where did I come from? Where am I going? What is the meaning of life? What is right? What is wrong? Is there life after death? These are the primal questions of the soul. And left unanswered, such questions will steal our rest.

Only one other living creature has as much trouble resting as we do. Not dogs. They doze. Not bears. They hibernate. Cats invented the catnap, and the sloths slumber twenty hours a day. (So that's what I was rooming with my sophomore year in college.) Most animals know how to rest. There is one exception. These creatures are woolly, simpleminded, and slow. No, not husbands on Saturday—sheep! Sheep can't sleep.

For sheep to sleep, everything must be just right. No predators. No tension in the flock. No bugs in the air. No hunger in the belly.[4] Everything has to be just so.

Unfortunately, sheep cannot find safe pasture, nor can they spray insecticide, deal with the frictions, or find food. They need help. They need a shepherd to "lead them" and help them "lie down in green pastures." Without a shepherd, they can't rest.

Without a shepherd, neither can we.

In the second verse of the Twenty-third Psalm, David the poet becomes David the artist. His quill becomes a brush, his parchment a canvas, and his words paint a picture. A flock of sheep on folded legs, encircling a shepherd. Bellies nestled deep in the long shoots of grass. A still pond on one side, the watching shepherd on the other. "He makes me to lie down in green pastures; He leads me beside the still waters" (Ps. 23:2 NKJV).

Note the two pronouns preceding the two verbs. *He* makes me . . . *He* leads me . . .

Who is the active one? Who is in charge? The shepherd. The shepherd selects the trail and prepares the pasture. The sheep's job—our job—is to watch the shepherd. With our eyes on our Shepherd, we'll be able to get some sleep. "You will keep him in perfect peace, whose mind is stayed on You" (Isa. 26:3 NKJV).

May I show you something? Flip to the back of this book, and look at an empty page. When you look at it, what do you see? What you see is a white piece of paper. Now place a dot in the center of the sheet. Look at it again. Now what do you see? You see the dot, don't you? And isn't that our problem? We let the dark marks eclipse the white space.

We see the waves of the water rather than the Savior walking through them. We focus on our paltry provisions rather than on the One who can feed five thousand hungry people. We concentrate on the dark Fridays of crucifixion and miss the bright Sundays of resurrection.

Change your focus and relax.

And while you are at it, change your schedule and rest!

The other day my wife met a friend at a restaurant for coffee. The two entered the parking lot at the same time. When Denalyn stepped out of her car, she saw her friend waving her over. Denalyn thought she was saying something, but she couldn't hear a word. A jack-hammer was pounding pavement only a few feet away. She walked toward her friend, who, as it turned out, was just saying hello, and the two entered the restaurant.

When it came time to leave, my wife couldn't find her keys. She looked in her purse, on the floor, in her friend's car. Finally when she went to her car, there they were. Not only were the keys in the ignition, the car was running. It had been running the entire time she and her friend were in the café.

Denalyn blames the oversight on the noise. "Everything was so loud, I forgot to turn it off."

The world gets that way. Life can get so loud we forget to shut it down. Maybe that's why God made such a big deal about rest in the Ten Commandments.

Since you did so well on the dot exercise, let me give you another. Of the ten declarations carved in the tablets, which one occupies the most space? Murder? Adultery? Stealing? You'd think so. Certainly each is worthy of ample coverage. But curiously, these commands are tributes to brevity. God needed only five English words to condemn adultery and four to denounce thievery and murder.

But when he came to the topic of rest, one sentence would not suffice.

Remember the Sabbath day, to keep it holy. Six days you shall labor and do all your work, but the seventh day is the Sabbath of the LORD your God. In it you shall do no work: you, nor your son, nor your daughter, nor your manservant, nor your maidservant, nor your cattle, nor your stranger who is within your gates. For in six days the LORD made the heavens and the earth, the sea, and all that is in them, and rested the seventh day. Therefore the LORD blessed the Sabbath day and hallowed it. (Exod. 20:8–11 NKJV)

God knows us so well. He can see the store owner reading this verse and thinking, "Somebody needs to work that day. If I can't, my son will." So God says, *Nor your son.* "Then my daughter will." *Nor your daughter.* "Then maybe an employee." *Nor them.* "I guess I'll have to send my cow to run the store, or maybe I'll find some stranger to help me." *No,* God says. *One day of the week you will say no to work and yes to worship. You will slow and sit down and lie down and rest.*

Still we object. "But . . . but . . . but . . . who is going to run the store?" "What about my grades?" "I've got my sales quota." We offer up one reason after another, but God silences them all with a poignant reminder: "In six days the LORD made the heavens and the earth, the sea, and all that is in them, and rested the seventh day." God's message is plain: "If creation didn't crash when I rested, it won't crash when you do."

Repeat these words after me: It is not my job to run the world.

A century ago Charles Spurgeon gave this advice to his preaching students:

Even beasts of burden must be turned out to grass occasionally; the very sea pauses at ebb and flood; earth keeps the Sabbath of the wintry months; and man, even when exalted to God's ambassador, must rest or faint, must trim his lamp or let it burn low; must recruit his vigor or grow prematurely old. . . . In the long run we shall do more by sometimes doing less.[5]

The bow cannot always be bent without fear of breaking. For a field to bear fruit, it must occasionally lie fallow. And for you to be healthy, you must rest. Slow down, and God will heal you. He will bring rest to your mind, to your body, and most of all to your soul. He will lead you to green pastures.

Green pastures were not the natural terrain of Judea. The hills around Bethlehem where David kept his flock were not lush and green. Even today they are white and parched. Any green pasture in Judea is the work of some shepherd. He has cleared the rough, rocky land. Stumps have been torn out, and brush has been burned. Irrigation. Cultivation. Such are the work of a shepherd.

Hence, when David says, "He makes me to lie down in green pastures," he is saying, "My shepherd makes me lie down in his finished work." With his own pierced hands, Jesus created a pasture for the soul. He tore out the thorny underbrush of condemnation. He pried loose the huge boulders of sin. In their place he planted seeds of grace and dug ponds of mercy.

And he invites us to rest there. Can you imagine the satisfaction in the heart of the shepherd when, with work completed, he sees his sheep rest in the tender grass?

Can you imagine the satisfaction in the heart of God when we do the same? His pasture is his gift to us. This is not a pasture that you have made. Nor is it a pasture that you deserve. It is a gift of God. "For it is by grace you have been saved, through faith—and this not from yourselves, it is the gift of God" (Eph. 2:8 NIV).

In a world rocky with human failure, there is a land lush with divine mercy. Your Shepherd invites you there. He wants you to lie down. Nestle deeply until you are hidden, buried, in the tall shoots of his love, and there you will find rest.

6

Whaddifs and Howells

The Burden of Worry

He leads me beside the still waters.

Psalm 23:2 nkjv

Y our ten-year-old is worried. So anxious he can't eat. So worried he can't sleep. "What's wrong?" you inquire. He shakes his head and moans, "I don't even have a pension plan."

Or your four-year-old is crying in bed. "What's wrong, sweetheart?" She whimpers, "I'll never pass college chemistry."

Your eight-year-old's face is stress-struck. "I'll be a rotten parent. What if I set a poor example for my kids?"

How would you respond to such statements? Besides calling a child psychologist, your response would be emphatic: "You're too young to worry about those things. When the time comes, you'll know what to do."

Fortunately, most kids don't have such thoughts.

Unfortunately, we adults have more than our share. Worry is the burlap bag of burdens. It's overflowing with "whaddifs" and "howells." "Whaddif it rains at my wedding?" "Howell I know when to discipline my kids?" "Whaddif I marry a guy who snores?" "Howell we pay our baby's tuition?" "Whaddif, after all my dieting, they learn that lettuce is fattening and chocolate isn't?"

The burlap bag of worry. Cumbersome. Chunky. Unattractive. Scratchy. Hard to get a handle on. Irritating to carry and impossible to give away. No one wants your worries.

The truth be told, you don't want them either. No one has to remind you of the high cost of anxiety. (But I will anyway.) Worry divides the mind. The biblical word for *worry (merimnao)* is a compound of two Greek words, *merizo* ("to divide") and *nous* ("the mind"). Anxiety splits our energy between today's priorities and tomorrow's problems. Part of our mind is on the now; the rest is on the not yet. The result is half-minded living.

That's not the only result. Worrying is not a disease, but it causes diseases. It has been connected to high blood pressure, heart trouble, blindness, migraine headaches, thyroid malfunctions, and a host of stomach disorders.

Anxiety is an expensive habit. Of course, it might be worth the cost if it worked. But it doesn't. Our frets are futile. Jesus said, "You cannot add any time to your life by worrying about it" (Matt. 6:27). Worry has never brightened a day, solved a problem, or cured a disease.

How can a person deal with anxiety? You might try what one fellow did. He worried so much that he decided to hire someone to do his worrying for him. He found a man who agreed to be his hired worrier for a salary of $200,000 per year. After the man accepted the job, his first question to his boss was, "Where are you going to get $200,000 per year?" To which the man responded, "That's your worry."

Sadly, worrying is one job you can't farm out, but you can overcome it. There is no better place to begin than in verse two of the shepherd's psalm.

"He leads me beside the still waters," David declares. And, in case we missed the point, he repeats the phrase in the next verse: "He leads me in the paths of righteousness."

"He leads me." God isn't behind me, yelling, "Go!" He is ahead of me, bidding, "Come!" He is in front, clearing the path, cutting the brush, showing the way. Just before the curve, he says, "Turn here."

Prior to the rise, he motions, "Step up here." Standing next to the rocks, he warns, "Watch your step here."

He leads us. He tells us what we need to know when we need to know it. As a New Testament writer would affirm: "We will find grace to help us *when we need it*" (Heb. 4:16 NLT, emphasis mine).

Listen to a different translation: "Let us therefore boldly approach the throne of our gracious God, where we may receive mercy and in his grace find *timely help*" (Heb. 4:16 NEB, emphasis mine).

God's help is timely. He helps us the same way a father gives plane tickets to his family. When I travel with my kids, I carry all our tickets in my satchel. When the moment comes to board the plane, I stand between the attendant and the child. As each daughter passes, I place a ticket in her hand. She, in turn, gives the ticket to the attendant. Each one receives the ticket in the nick of time.

What I do for my daughters God does for you. He places himself between you and the need. And at the right time, he gives you the ticket. Wasn't this the promise he gave his disciples? "When you are arrested and judged, don't worry ahead of time about what you should say. Say whatever *is given you to say at that time,* because it will not really be you speaking; it will be the Holy Spirit" (Mark 13:11, emphasis mine).

Isn't this the message God gave the children of Israel? He promised to supply them with manna each day. But he told them to collect only one day's supply at a time. Those who disobeyed and collected enough for two days found themselves with rotten manna. The only exception to the rule was the day prior to the Sabbath. On Friday they could gather twice as much. Otherwise, God would give them what they needed, in their time of need.

God leads us. God will do the right thing at the right time. And what a difference that makes.

Since I know his provision is timely, I can enjoy the present.

"Give your entire attention to what God is doing right now, and don't get worked up about what may or may not happen tomorrow. God will help you deal with whatever hard things come up when the time comes" (Matt. 6:34 MSG).

That last phrase is worthy of your highlighter: "when the time comes."

"I don't know what I'll do if my husband dies." You will, *when the time comes.*

"When my children leave the house, I don't think I can take it." It won't be easy, but strength will arrive *when the time comes.*

"I could never lead a church. There is too much I don't know." You may be right. Or you may be wanting to know everything too soon. Could it be that God will reveal answers to you *when the time comes?*

The key is this: Meet today's problems with today's strength. Don't start tackling tomorrow's problems until tomorrow. You do not have tomorrow's strength yet. You simply have enough for today.

More than eighty years ago a great Canadian man of medicine, Sir William Osler, delivered a speech to the students of Yale University entitled "A Way of Life." In the message he related an event that occurred while he was aboard an ocean liner.

One day while he was visiting with the ship's captain, a loud, piercing alarm sounded, followed by strange grinding and crashing sounds below the deck. "Those are our watertight compartments closing," the captain explained. "It's an important part of our safety drill. In case of real trouble, water leaking into one compartment would not affect the rest of the ship. Even if we should collide with an iceberg, as did the *Titanic,* water rushing in will fill only that particular ruptured compartment. The ship, however, will still remain afloat."

When he spoke to the students at Yale, Osler remembered the captain's description of the boat:

> Each one of you is certainly a much more marvelous organization than that great liner and bound on a far longer voyage. What I urge is that you learn to master your life by living each day in a day-tight compartment and this will certainly ensure your safety throughout your entire journey of life. Touch a button and hear, at every level of your life, the iron doors shutting out the Past—the dead yesterdays. Touch another and shut off, with a metal curtain, the Future—the unborn tomorrows. Then you are safe—safe for today.
>
> Think not of the amount to be accomplished, the difficulties to be overcome, but set earnestly at the little task near your elbow, letting that be sufficient for the day; for surely our plain duty is not to see what lies dimly at a distance but to do what lies clearly at hand.[1]

Jesus made the same point in fewer words: "So don't worry about tomorrow, because tomorrow will have its own worries. Each day has enough trouble of its own" (Matt. 6:34).

Easy to say. Not always easy to do, right? We are so prone to worry. Just last night I was worrying in my sleep. I dreamed that I was diagnosed with ALS, a degenerative muscle disease, which took the life of my father. I awakened from the dream and, right there in the middle of the night, began to worry. Then Jesus' words came to my mind, "Don't worry about tomorrow." And for once, I decided not to. I dropped the burlap sack. After all, why let tomorrow's imaginary problem rob tonight's rest? Can I prevent the disease by staying awake? Will I postpone the affliction by thinking about it? Of course not. So I did the most spiritual thing I could have done. I went back to sleep.

Why don't you do the same? God is leading you. Leave tomorrow's problems until tomorrow.

Arthur Hays Sulzberger was the publisher of the *New York Times* during the Second World War. Because of the world conflict, he found it almost impossible to sleep. He was never able to banish worries from his mind until he adopted as his motto these five words—"one step enough for me"—taken from the hymn "Lead Kindly Light."[2]

> Lead, kindly Light . . .
> Keep Thou my feet; I do not ask to see
> The distant scene; one step enough for me.

God isn't going to let you see the distant scene either. So you might as well quit looking for it. He promises a lamp unto our feet, not a crystal ball into the future.[3] We do not need to know what will happen tomorrow. We only need to know he leads us and "we will find grace to help us when we need it" (Heb. 4:16 NLT).

7

It's a Jungle Out There

The Burden of Hopelessness

He restores my soul.

PSALM 23:3 NKJV

I wonder if you could imagine yourself in a jungle. A dense jungle. A dark jungle. Your friends convinced you it was time for a once-in-a-lifetime trip, and here you are. You paid the fare. You crossed the ocean. You hired the guide and joined the group. And you ventured where you had never ventured before— into the thick, strange world of the jungle.

Sound interesting? Let's take it a step farther. Imagine that you are in the jungle, lost and alone. You paused to lace your boot, and when you looked up, no one was near. You took a chance and went to the right; now you're wondering if the others went to the left. (Or did you go left and they go right?)

Whatever, you are alone. And you have been alone for, well, you don't know how long it has been. Your watch was attached to your pack, and your pack is on the shoulder of the nice guy from New Jersey who volunteered to hold it while you tied your boots. You didn't intend for him to walk off with it. But he did. And here you are, stuck in the middle of nowhere.

You have a problem. First, you were not made for this place. Drop you in the center of avenues and buildings, and you could sniff your way home. But here in sky-blocking foliage? Here in trail-hiding thickets? You are out of your element. You weren't made for this jungle.

What's worse, you aren't equipped. You have no machete. No knife.

No matches. No flares. No food. You aren't equipped, but now you are trapped—and you haven't a clue how to get out.

Sound like fun to you? Me either. Before moving on, let's pause and ask how you would feel. Given such circumstances, what emotions would surface? With what thoughts would you wrestle?

Fear? Of course you would.

Anxiety? To say the least.

Anger? I could understand that. (You'd like to get your hands on those folks who convinced you to take this trip.)

But most of all, what about hopelessness? No idea where to turn. No hunch what to do. Who could blame you for sitting on a log (better check for snakes first), burying your face in your hands, and thinking, *I'll never get out of here.* You have no direction, no equipment, no hope.

Can you freeze frame that emotion for a moment? Can you sense, for just a second, how it feels to be out of your element? Out of solutions? Out of ideas and energy? Can you imagine, just for a moment, how it feels to be out of hope?

If you can, you can relate to many people in this world.

For many people, life is—well, life is a jungle. Not a jungle of trees and beasts. Would that it were so simple. Would that our jungles could be cut with a machete or our adversaries trapped in a cage. But our jungles are comprised of the thicker thickets of failing health, broken hearts, and empty wallets. Our forests are framed with hospital walls and divorce courts. We don't hear the screeching of birds or the roaring of lions, but we do hear the complaints of neighbors and the demands of bosses. Our predators are our creditors, and the brush that surrounds us is the rush that exhausts us.

It's a jungle out there.

And for some, even for many, hope is in short supply. Hopelessness is an odd bag. Unlike the others, it isn't full. It is empty, and its emptiness creates the burden. Unzip the top and examine all the pockets. Turn it upside down and shake it hard. The bag of hopelessness is painfully empty.

Not a very pretty picture, is it? Let's see if we can brighten it up. We've imagined the emotions of being lost; you think we can do the same with being rescued? What would it take to restore your hope? What would you need to reenergize your journey?

Though the answers are abundant, three come quickly to mind.

The first would be a person. Not just any person. You don't need someone equally confused. You need someone who knows the way out.

And from him you need some vision. You need someone to lift your spirits. You need someone to look you in the face and say, "This isn't the end. Don't give up. There is a better place than this. And I'll lead you there."

And, perhaps most important, you need direction. If you have only a person but no renewed vision, all you have is company. If he has a vision but no direction, you have a dreamer for company. But if you have a person with direction—who can take you from this place to the right place—ah, then you have one who can restore your hope.

Or, to use David's words, "He restores my soul."

Our Shepherd majors in restoring hope to the soul. Whether you are a lamb lost on a craggy ledge or a city slicker alone in a deep jungle, everything changes when your rescuer appears.

Your loneliness diminishes, because you have fellowship.

Your despair decreases, because you have vision.

Your confusion begins to lift, because you have direction.

Please note: You haven't left the jungle. The trees still eclipse the sky, and the thorns still cut the skin. Animals lurk and rodents scurry. The jungle is still a jungle. It hasn't changed, but you have. You have changed because you have hope. And you have hope because you have met someone who can lead you out.

Your Shepherd knows that you were not made for this place. He knows you are not equipped for this place. So he has come to guide you out.

He has come to restore your soul. He is the perfect one to do so.

He has the right vision. He reminds you that "you are like foreigners and strangers in this world" (1 Pet. 2:11). And he urges you to lift your eyes from the jungle around you to the heaven above you. "Don't shuffle along, eyes to the ground, absorbed with the things right in front of you. Look up, and be alert to what is going on around Christ. . . . See things from his perspective" (Col. 3:2 MSG).

David said it this way, "I lift up my eyes to the hills—where does my help come from? My help comes from the LORD, the Maker of heaven and earth. He will not let your foot slip—he who watches over you will not slumber. . . . The LORD watches over you . . . the sun will not harm you by day, nor the moon by night. The LORD will keep you from all harm—he will watch over your life" (Ps. 121:1–7 NIV).

God, your rescuer, has the right vision. He also has the right direction. He made the boldest claim in the history of man when he declared, "I am the way" (John 14:6). People wondered if the claim was accurate. He answered their questions by cutting a path through the underbrush of sin and death . . . and escaping alive. He's the only One who ever did. And he is the only One who can help you and me do the same.

He has the right vision: He has seen the homeland. He has the right directions: He has cut the path. But most of all, he is the right person, for he is our God. Who knows the jungle better than the One who made it? And who knows the pitfalls of the path better than the One who has walked it?

The story is told of a man on an African safari deep in the jungle. The guide before him had a machete and was whacking away the tall weeds and thick underbrush. The traveler, wearied and hot, asked in frustration, "Where are we? Do you know where you are taking me? Where is the path?!" The seasoned guide stopped and looked back at the man and replied, "I am the path."

We ask the same questions, don't we? We ask God, "Where are you taking me? Where is the path?" And he, like the guide, doesn't tell us. Oh, he may give us a hint or two, but that's all. If he did, would we understand? Would we comprehend our location? No, like the traveler, we are unacquainted with this jungle. So rather than give us an answer, Jesus gives us a far greater gift. He gives us himself.

Does he remove the jungle? No, the vegetation is still thick.

Does he purge the predators? No, danger still lurks

Jesus doesn't give hope by changing the jungle; he restores our hope by giving us himself. And he has promised to stay until the very end. "I am with you always, to the very end of the age" (Matt. 28:20 NIV).

We need that reminder. We all need that reminder. For all of us need hope.

Some of you don't need it right now. Your jungle has become a meadow and your journey a delight. If such is the case, congratulations. But remember—we do not know what tomorrow holds. We do not know where this road will lead. You may be one turn from a cemetery, from a hospital bed, from an empty house. You may be a bend in the road from a jungle.

And though you don't need your hope restored today, you may tomorrow. And you need to know to whom to turn.

Or perhaps you do need hope today. You know you were not made for this place. You know you are not equipped. You want someone to lead you out.

If so, call out for your Shepherd. He knows your voice. And he's just waiting for your request.

8

A Heavenly Exchange

The Burden of Guilt

He leads me in the paths of righteousness for His name's sake.

PSALM 23:3 NKJV

A friend organized a Christmas cookie swap for our church office staff. The plan was simple. Price of admission was a tray of cookies. Your tray entitled you to pick cookies from the other trays. You could leave with as many cookies as you brought.

Sounds simple, if you know how to cook. But what if you can't? What if you can't tell a pan from a pot? What if, like me, you are culinarily challenged? What if you're as comfortable in an apron as a bodybuilder in a tutu? If such is the case, you've got a problem.

Such was the case, and I had a problem. I had no cookies to bring; hence I would have no place at the party. I would be left out, turned away, shunned, eschewed, and dismissed. (Are you feeling sorry for me yet?)

This was my plight.

And, forgive me for bringing it up, but your plight's even worse.

God is planning a party . . . a party to end all parties. Not a cookie party, but a feast. Not giggles and chitchat in the conference room, but wide-eyed wonder in the throne room of God.

Yes, the guestlist is impressive. Your question to Jonah about undergoing a gut check in a fish gut? You'll be able to ask him. But more impressive than the names of the guests is the nature of the guests. No egos, no power plays. Guilt, shame, and sorrow will be checked at the gate. Disease, death, and depression will be the Black Plagues of a distant past. What we now see daily, there we will never see.

And what we now see vaguely, there we will see clearly. We will see God. Not by faith. Not through the eyes of Moses or Abraham or David. Not via Scripture or sunsets or summer rains. We will see not God's work or words, but we will see him! For he is not the host of the party; he is the party. His goodness is the banquet. His voice is the music. His radiance is the light, and his love is the endless topic of discussion.

There is only one hitch. The price of admission is somewhat steep. In order to come to the party, you need to be righteous. Not good. Not decent. Not a taxpayer or churchgoer.

Citizens of heaven are righteous. R-i-g-h-t.

All of us *occasionally* do what is right. A few *predominantly* do what is right. But do any of us *always* do what is right? According to Paul we don't. "There is none righteous, no, not one" (Rom. 3:10 NKJV).

Paul is adamant about this. He goes on to say, "No one anywhere has kept on doing what is right; not one" (Rom. 3:12 TLB).

Some may beg to differ. "I'm not perfect, Max, but I'm better than most folks. I've led a good life. I don't break the rules. I don't break hearts. I help people. I like people. Compared to others, I think I could say I'm a righteous person."

I used to try that one on my mother. She'd tell me my room wasn't clean, and I'd ask her to go with me to my brother's room. His was always messier than mine. "Now my room is clean; just look at his."

Never worked. She'd walk me down the hall to her room. When it came to tidy rooms, my mom was righteous. Her closet was just right. Her bed was just right. Her bathroom was just right. Compared to hers, my room was, well, just wrong. She would show me her room and say, "This is what I mean by clean."

God does the same. He points to himself and says, "This is what I mean by righteousness."

Righteousness is who God is.

"Our God and Savior Jesus Christ does what is right" (2 Pet. 1:1).

"God is a righteous judge" (Ps. 7:11 NIV).

"The LORD is righteous, he loves justice" (Ps. 11:7 NIV).

God's righteousness "endures forever" (Ps. 112:3 NIV) and "reaches to the skies" (Ps. 71:19 NIV).

Isaiah described God as "a righteous God and a Savior" (Isa. 45:21 NIV).

On the eve of his death, Jesus began his prayer with the words "Righteous Father" (John 17:25 NIV).

Get the point? God is righteous. His decrees are righteous (Rom. 1:32). His judgment is righteous (Rom. 2:5). His requirements are righteous (Rom. 8:4). His acts are righteous (Dan. 9:16). Daniel declared, "Our God is right in everything he does" (Dan. 9:14).

God is never wrong. He has never rendered a wrong decision, experienced the wrong attitude, taken the wrong path, said the wrong thing, or acted the wrong way. He is never too late or too early, too loud or too soft, too fast or too slow. He has always been and always will be right. He is righteous.

When it comes to righteousness, God runs the table without so much as a bank shot. And when it comes to righteousness, we don't know which end of the cue stick to hold. Hence, our plight.

Will God, who is righteous, spend eternity with those who are not? Would Harvard admit a third-grade dropout? If it did, the act might be benevolent, but it wouldn't be right. If God accepted the unrighteous, the invitation would be even nicer, but would he be right? Would he be right to overlook our sins? Lower his standards? No. He wouldn't be right. And if God is anything, he is right.

He told Isaiah that righteousness would be his plumb line, the standard by which his house is measured (Isa. 28:17). If we are unrighteous, then, we are left in the hallway with no cookies. Or to use Paul's analogy, "we're sinners, every one of us, in the same sinking boat with everybody else" (Rom. 3:19 MSG). Then what are we to do?

Carry a load of guilt? Many do. So many do.

What if our spiritual baggage were visible? Suppose the luggage in our hearts was literal luggage on the street. You know what you'd see most of all? Suitcases of guilt. Bags bulging with binges, blowups, and compromises. Look around you. The fellow in the gray-flannel suit? He's dragging a decade of regrets. The kid with the baggy jeans and nose ring? He'd give anything to retract the words he said to his mother. But he can't. So he tows them along. The woman in the business suit? Looks as if she could run for senator? She'd rather run for help, but she can't run at all. Not hauling that carpetbag of cagmag everywhere she goes.

Listen. The weight of weariness pulls you down. Self-reliance misleads you. Disappointments discourage you. Anxiety plagues you. But guilt? Guilt consumes you.

So what do we do? Our Lord is right, and we are wrong. His party is for the guiltless, and we are anything but. What do we do?

I can tell you what I did. I confessed my need. Remember my cookie dilemma? This is the e-mail I sent to the whole staff. "I can't cook, so I can't be at the party."

Did any of the assistants have mercy on me? No.

Did any of the staff have mercy on me? No.

Did any of the Supreme Court justices have mercy upon me? No.

But a saintly sister in the church did have mercy on me. How she heard of my problem, I do not know. Perhaps my name found its way on an emergency prayer list. But I do know this. Only moments before the celebration, I was given a gift, a plate of cookies, twelve circles of kindness.

And by virtue of that gift, I was privileged a place at the party.

Did I go? You bet your cookies I did. Like a prince carrying a crown on a pillow, I carried my gift into the room, set it on the table, and stood tall. And because some good soul heard my plea, I was given a place at the table.

And because God hears your plea, you'll be given the same. Only, he did more—oh, so much more—than bake cookies for you.

It was, at once, history's most beautiful and most horrible moment. Jesus stood in the tribunal of heaven. Sweeping a hand over all creation, he pleaded, "Punish me for their mistakes. See the murderer? Give me his penalty. The adulteress? I'll take her shame. The bigot, the liar, the thief? Do to me what you would do to them. Treat me as you would a sinner."

And God did. "For Christ died for sins once for all, the righteous for the unrighteous, to bring you to God" (1 Pet. 3:18 NIV).

Yes, righteousness is what God is, and, yes, righteousness is what we are not, and, yes, righteousness is what God requires. But "God has a way to make people right with him" (Rom. 3:21).

David said it like this: "He leads me in the paths of righteousness" (Ps. 23:3 NKJV).

The path of righteousness is a narrow, winding trail up a steep hill. At the top of the hill is a cross. At the base of the cross are bags. Countless bags full of innumerable sins. Calvary is the compost pile for guilt. Would you like to leave yours there as well?

One final thought about the Christmas cookie party. Did everyone know I didn't cook the cookies? If they didn't, I told them. I told them I was present by virtue of someone else's work. My only contribution was my own confession.

We'll be saying the same for eternity.

9

Get Over Yourself

The Burden of Arrogance

For His name's sake . . .

PSALM 23:3 NKJV

H umility is such an elusive virtue. Once you think you have it, you don't, or you wouldn't think you did. You've heard the story of the boy who received the "Most Humble" badge and had it taken away because he wore it?

Something similar happened to me just the other morning. I had retreated to a nearby town to work on this book. The village is a perfect hideaway; it is quaint, quiet, and has great food.

I'd gone to a café for breakfast when I noticed that people were staring at me. As I parked, two fellows turned and looked in my direction. A woman did a double take as I entered, and several patrons looked up as I passed. When I took my seat, the waitress gave me a menu but not before she'd given me a good study.

Why the attention? Couldn't be my fly; I was wearing sweats. After some thought I took the mature posture and assumed they recognized me from my book jackets. *Why, this must be a town of readers. And, I* shrugged to myself, *they know a good author when they see one.* My appreciation for the village only increased.

Giving a smile to the folks at the other tables, I set about to enjoy my meal. When I walked to the cash register, the heads turned again. *I'm sure Steinbeck had the same problem.* The woman who took my money started to say something but then paused. Overwhelmed, I guessed.

It was only when I stopped in the rest room that I saw the real reason for the attention—a ribbon of dried blood on my chin. My patch job on the shaving nick hadn't worked, and I was left with my own turkey wattle.

So much for feeling famous. They probably thought I was an escapee from a Texas prison.

Oh, the things God does to keep us humble. He does it for our own good, you know. Would you set a saddle on the back of your five-year-old? Would God let you be saddled with arrogance? No way.

This is one piece of luggage God hates. He doesn't dislike arrogance. He doesn't disapprove of arrogance. He's not unfavorably disposed toward arrogance. God hates arrogance. What a meal of maggots does for our stomach, human pride does for God's.

"I hate pride and arrogance" (Prov. 8:13 NIV).

"The LORD despises pride" (Prov. 16:5 NLT).

God says, "Do nothing out of . . . vain conceit" (Phil. 2:3 NIV). And, "Do not let arrogance come out of your mouth" (1 Sam. 2:3 NASB). And, in the same way that he gives grace to the humble, "God opposes the proud" (1 Pet. 5:5 NIV). As humility goes before honor, "pride goes . . . before a fall" (Prov. 16:18 NIV).

Ever wonder why churches are powerful in one generation but empty the next? Perhaps the answer is found in Proverbs 15:25: "The LORD will tear down the house of the proud" (NASB).

God hates arrogance. He hates arrogance because we haven't done anything to be arrogant about. Do art critics give awards to the canvas? Is there a Pulitzer for ink? Can you imagine a scalpel growing smug after a successful heart transplant? Of course not. They are only tools, so they get no credit for the accomplishments.

And the message of the Twenty-third Psalm is that we have nothing to be proud about either. We have rest, salvation, blessings, and a home in heaven—and we did nothing to earn any of it. Who did? Who did the work? The answer threads through the psalm like a silk thread through pearls.

"He makes me . . ."

"He leads me . . ."

"He restores my soul . . ."

"You are with me . . ."

"Your rod and Your staff . . . comfort me . . ."

"You prepare a table . . ."

"You anoint my head . . ."

We may be the canvas, the paper, or the scalpel, but we are not the ones who deserve the applause. And just to make sure we get the point, right smack-dab in the middle of the poem, David declares who does. The shepherd leads his sheep, not for our names' sake, but "for His name's sake."

Why does God have anything to do with us? *For his name's sake.* No other name on the marquee. No other name up in lights. No other name on the front page. This is all done for God's glory.

Why? What's the big deal? Does God have an ego problem?

No, but we do. We are about as responsible with applause as I was with the cake I won in the first grade. In the grand finale of the musical chairs competition, guess who had a seat? And guess what the little red-headed, freckle-faced boy won? A tender, moist coconut cake. And guess what the boy wanted to do that night in one sitting? Eat the whole thing! Not half of it. Not a piece of it. All of it! After all, I'd won it.

But you know what my folks did? They rationed the cake. They gave me only what I could handle. Knowing that today's binge is tomorrow's bellyache, they made sure I didn't get sick on my success.

God does the same. He takes the cake. He takes the credit, not because he needs it, but because he knows we can't handle it. We aren't content with a bite of adulation; we tend to swallow it all. It messes with our systems. The praise swells our heads and shrinks our brains, and pretty soon we start thinking we had something to do with our survival. Pretty soon we forget we were made out of dirt and rescued from sin.

Pretty soon we start praying like the fellow at the religious caucus: "God, I thank you that the world has people like me. The man on the corner needs welfare—I don't. The prostitute on the street has AIDS—I don't. The drunk at the bar needs alcohol—I don't. The gay caucus needs morality—I don't. I thank you that the world has people like me."

Fortunately, there was a man in the same meeting who had deflected all the applause. Too contrite even to look to the skies, he bowed and prayed, "God, have mercy on me, a sinner. Like my brother on welfare, I'm dependent on your grace. Like my sister with AIDS, I'm infected with mistakes. Like my friend who drinks, I need something to ease my pain. And as you love and give direction to the gay, grant some to me as well. Have mercy on me, a sinner."

After telling a story like that, Jesus said, "I tell you, when this man went home, he was right with God, but the Pharisee was not. All who make themselves great will be made humble, but all who make themselves humble will be made great" (Luke 18:14).

With the same intensity that he hates arrogance, God loves humility. The Jesus who said, "I am gentle and humble in heart" (Matt. 11:29 NASB) loves those who are gentle and humble in heart. "Though the LORD is supreme, he takes care of those who are humble" (Ps. 138:6). God says, "I live with people who are . . . humble" (Isa. 57:15). He also says, "To this one I will look, to him who is humble and contrite" (Isa. 66:2 NASB). And to the humble, God gives great treasures:

He gives honor: "Humility goes before honor" (Prov. 15:33 NRSV).

He gives wisdom: "With the humble is wisdom" (Prov. 11:2 NASB).

He gives direction: "He teaches the humble His way" (Ps. 25:9 NASB).

And most significantly, he gives grace: "God . . . gives grace to the humble" (1 Pet. 5:5).

And this reassurance: "He crowns the humble with salvation" (Ps. 149:4 NIV).

The mightiest of the saints were known for their humility. Though Moses had served as prince of Egypt and emancipator of the slaves, the Bible says, "Moses was . . . more humble than anyone else" (Num. 12:3 NIV).

The apostle Paul was saved through a personal visit from Jesus. He was carried into the heavens and had the ability to raise the dead. But when he introduced himself, he mentioned none of these. He simply said, "I, Paul, am God's slave" (Titus 1:1 MSG).

John the Baptist was a blood relative of Jesus and the first evangelist in history, but he is remembered in Scripture as the one who resolved, "He must increase, but I must decrease" (John 3:30 NKJV).

God loves humility. Could that be the reason he offers so many tips on cultivating it? May I, ahem, humbly articulate a few?

1. *Assess yourself honestly.* Humility isn't the same as low self-esteem. Being humble doesn't mean you think you have nothing to offer; it means you know exactly what you have to offer and no more. "Don't cherish exaggerated ideas of yourself or your importance, but try to have a sane estimate of your capabilities by the light of the faith that God has given to you" (Rom. 12:3 PHILLIPS).

2. *Don't take success too seriously.* Scripture gives this warning: "When your . . . silver and gold increase, . . . your heart will become proud" (Deut. 8:13–14). Counteract this pride with reminders of the brevity of life and the frailty of wealth.

Ponder your success and count your money in a cemetery, and remember that neither of the two is buried with you. "People come into this world with nothing, and when they die they leave with nothing" (Eccles. 5:15). I saw a reminder of this in a cemetery. Parked next to the entrance was a nice recreational boat with a For Sale sign. You had to wonder if the fisherman realized he couldn't take it with him.

3. *Celebrate the significance of others.* "In humility consider others better than yourselves" (Phil. 2:3 NIV). Columnist Rick Reilly gave this advice to rookie professional athletes: "Stop thumping your chest. The line blocked, the quarterback threw you a perfect spiral while getting his head knocked off, and the *good* receiver blew the double coverage. Get over yourself."[1]

The truth is, every touchdown in life is a team effort. Applaud your teammates. An elementary-age boy came home from the tryouts for the school play. "Mommy, Mommy," he announced, "I got a part. I've been chosen to sit in the audience and clap and cheer." When you have a chance to clap and cheer, do you take it? If you do, your head is starting to fit your hat size.

4. *Don't demand your own parking place.* This was the instruction of Jesus to his followers: "Go sit in a seat that is not important. When the host comes to you, he may say, 'Friend, move up here to a more important place.' Then all the other guests will respect you" (Luke 14:10).

Demanding respect is like chasing a butterfly. Chase it, and you'll never catch it. Sit still, and it may light on your shoulder. The French philosopher Blaise Pascal asked, "Do you wish people to speak well of you? Then never speak well of yourself."[2] Maybe that's why the Bible says, "Don't praise yourself. Let someone else do it" (Prov. 27:2).

5. *Never announce your success before it occurs.* Or as one of the kings of Israel said, "One who puts on his armor should not boast like one who takes it off" (1 Kings 20:11 NIV). Charles Spurgeon trained many young ministers. On one occasion a student stepped up to preach with great confidence but failed miserably. He came down, humbled and

meek. Spurgeon told him, "If you had gone up as you came down, you would have come down as you went up."[3] If humility precedes an event, then confidence may follow.

6. Speak humbly. "Let no arrogance come from your mouth" (1 Sam. 2:3 NKJV). Don't be cocky. People aren't impressed with your opinions. Take a tip from Benjamin Franklin.

[I developed] the habit of expressing myself in terms of modest diffidence, never using when I advance any thing that may possibly be disputed, the words certainly, undoubtedly, or any others that give the air of positiveness to an opinion; but rather I say, I conceive or I apprehend a thing to be so or so. . . . This habit I believe has been a great advantage to me.[4]

It would be a great advantage to us as well.

One last thought to foster humility.

7. Live at the foot of the cross. Paul said, "The cross of our Lord Jesus Christ is my only reason for bragging" (Gal. 6:14). Do you feel a need for affirmation? Does your self-esteem need attention? You don't need to drop names or show off. You need only pause at the base of the cross and be reminded of this: The maker of the stars would rather die for you than live without you. And that is a fact. So if you need to brag, brag about that.

And check your chin occasionally.

I Will Lead You Home

The Burden of the Grave

Yea, though I walk through the valley of the shadow
of death, I will fear no evil; for You are with me;
Your rod and Your staff, they comfort me.

PSALM 23:4 NKJV

S ummer in ancient Palestine. A woolly bunch of bobbing heads follow the shepherd out of the gate. The morning sun has scarcely crested the horizon, and he is already leading his flock. Like every other day, he guides them through the gate and out into the fields. But unlike most days, the shepherd will not return home tonight. He will not rest on his bed, and the sheep will not sleep in their fenced-in pasture. This is the day the shepherd takes the sheep to the high country. Today he leads his flock to the mountains.

He has no other choice. Springtime grazing has left his pasture bare, so he must seek new fields. With no companion other than his sheep and no desire other than their welfare, he leads them to the deep grass of the hillsides. The shepherd and his flock will be gone for weeks, perhaps months. They will stay well into the autumn, until the grass is gone and the chill is unbearable.

Not all shepherds make this journey. The trek is long. The path is dangerous. Poisonous plants can infect the flock. Wild animals can attack the flock. There are narrow trails and dark valleys. Some shepherds choose the security of the barren pasture below.

But the good shepherd doesn't. He knows the path. He has walked this trail many times. Besides, he is prepared. Staff in hand

and rod attached to his belt. With his staff he will nudge the flock; with his rod he will protect and lead the flock. He will lead them to the mountains.

David understood this annual pilgrimage. Before he led Israel, he led sheep. And could his time as a shepherd be the inspiration behind one of the greatest verses in the Bible? "Yea, though I walk through the valley of the shadow of death, I will fear no evil; for You are with me; Your rod and Your staff, they comfort me" (Ps. 23:4 NKJV).

For what the shepherd does with the flock, our Shepherd will do with us. He will lead us to the high country. When the pasture is bare down here, God will lead us up there. He will guide us through the gate, out of the flatlands, and up the path of the mountain.

As one shepherd writes:

Every mountain has its valleys. Its sides are scarred by deep ravines and gulches and draws. And the best route to the top is always through these valleys.

Any sheepman familiar with the high country knows this. He leads his flock gently, but persistently up the paths that wind through the dark valleys.[1]

Someday our Shepherd will do the same with us. He will take us to the mountain by way of the valley. He will guide us to his house through the valley of the shadow of death.

Many years ago when I lived in Miami, our church office received a call from a nearby funeral home. A man had identified the body of an indigent as his brother and wanted a memorial service. He didn't know any ministers in the area. Would we say a few words? The senior minister and I agreed. When we arrived, the brother of the deceased had selected a text from a Spanish Bible: "Yea, though I walk through the valley of the shadow of death, I will fear no evil; for You are with me; Your rod and Your staff, they comfort me" (Ps. 23:4 NKJV).

He needed assurance that, though his brother had lived alone, he did not die alone. And for that assurance, he turned to this verse. You've likely done the same.

If you've attended a memorial service, you've heard the words. If you've walked through a cemetery, you've read them. They're quoted at the gravesides of paupers, carved on the headstones of kings. Those who know nothing of the Bible know this part of the Bible. Those who quote no scripture can remember this scripture, the one about the valley and the shadow and the shepherd.

Why? Why are these words so treasured? Why is this verse so beloved? I can think of a couple of reasons. By virtue of this psalm, David grants us two important reminders that can help us surrender our fear of the grave.

We all have to face it. In a life marked by doctor appointments, dentist appointments, and school appointments, there is one appointment that none of us will miss, the appointment with death. "Everyone must die once, and after that be judged by God" (Heb. 9:27 TEV). Oh, how we'd like to change that verse. Just a word or two would suffice. *"Nearly everyone must die . . ."* or *"Everyone but me must die . . ."* or *"Everyone who forgets to eat right and take vitamins must die . . ."* But those are not God's words. In his plan everyone must die, even those who eat right and take their vitamins.

I could have gone all day without reminding you of that. We do our best to avoid the topic. One wise man, however, urges us to face it squarely: "We all must die, and everyone living should think about this" (Eccles. 7:2). Solomon isn't promoting a morbid obsession with death. He is reminding us to be honest about the inevitable.

Moses gave the same exhortation. In the only psalm attributed to his pen, he prayed, "Teach us how short our lives really are so that we may be wise" (Ps. 90:12).

The wise remember the brevity of life. Exercise may buy us a few more heartbeats. Medicine may grant us a few more breaths. But in the end, there is an end. And the best way to face life is to be honest about death.

David was. He may have slain Goliath, but he had no illusions about sidestepping the giant of death. And though his first reminder sobers us, his second reminder encourages us: *We don't have to face death alone.*

Don't miss the shift in David's vocabulary. Up to this point, you and I have been the audience and God has been the topic. "The LORD is my shepherd." "He makes me to lie down." "He leads me beside the still waters." "He restores my soul." "He leads me in the paths of right-eousness." For the first three verses, David speaks to us and God listens.

But suddenly in verse four, David speaks to God and we listen. It's as if David's face, which was on us, now lifts toward God. His poem becomes a prayer. Rather than speak to us, he speaks to the Good Shepherd. "You are with me; Your rod and Your staff, they comfort me."

David's implied message is subtle but crucial. Don't face death with-out facing God. Don't even speak of death without speaking to God. He and he alone can guide you through the valley. Others may specu-late or aspire, but only God knows the way to get you home. And only God is committed to getting you there safely.

Years after David wrote these words, another Bethlehem Shepherd would say: "There are many rooms in my Father's house; I would not tell you this if it were not true. I am going there to prepare a place for you. After I go and prepare a place for you, I will come back and take you to be with me so that you may be where I am" (John 14:2–3).

Note the promise of Jesus. "I will come back and take you to be with me." He pledges to take us home. He does not delegate this task. He may send missionaries to teach you, angels to protect you, teachers to guide you, singers to inspire you, and physicians to heal you, but he sends no one to take you. He reserves this job for himself. "I will come back and take you home." He is your personal Shepherd. And he is personally responsible to lead you home. And because he is present when any of his sheep dies, you can say what David said, "I will fear no evil."

When my daughters were younger, we enjoyed many fun afternoons in the swimming pool. Just like all of us, they had to overcome their fears in order to swim. One of the final fears they had to face was the fear of the deep. It's one thing to swim on the surface; it's another to plunge down to the bottom. I mean, who knows what kind of dragons and serpents dwell in the depths of an eight-foot pool? You and I know there is no evil to fear, but a six-year-old doesn't. A child feels the same way about the deep that you and I feel about death. We aren't sure what awaits us down there.

I didn't want my daughters to be afraid of the deep end, so with each I played Shamu the whale. My daughter would be the trainer. I would be Shamu. She would pinch her nose and put her arm around my neck, then down we would go. Deep, deep, deep until we could touch the bottom of the pool. Then up we would explode, breaking the surface. After several plunges they realized they had nothing to fear. They feared no evil. Why? Because I was with them.

And when God calls us into the deep valley of death, he will be with us. Dare we think that he would abandon us in the moment of death? Would a father force his child to swim the deep alone? Would the shepherd require his sheep to journey to the highlands alone? Of course not. Would God require his child to journey to eternity alone? Absolutely not! He is with you!

What God said to Moses, he says to you: "My Presence will go with you, and I will give you rest" (Exod. 33:14 NIV).

What God said to Jacob, he says to you: "I am with you and will watch over you wherever you go" (Gen. 28:15 NIV).

What God said to Joshua, he says to you: "As I was with Moses, so I will be with you; I will never leave you nor forsake you" (Josh. 1:5 NIV).

What God said to the nation of Israel, he says to you: "When you pass through the waters, I will be with you" (Isa. 43:2 NIV).

The Good Shepherd is with you. And because he is with you, you can say what David said: "I will fear no evil; for You are with me; Your rod and Your staff, they comfort me."

Years ago a chaplain in the French army used the Twenty-third Psalm to encourage soldiers before battle. He would urge them to repeat the opening clause of the psalm, ticking it off, one finger at a time. The little finger represented the word *the;* the ring finger represented the word LORD; the middle finger, *is;* the index finger, *my;* and the thumb, *shepherd.* Then he asked every soldier to write the words on the palm of his hand and to repeat the verse whenever he needed strength.

The chaplain placed special emphasis on the message of the index finger—*my.* He reminded the soldiers that God is a personal shepherd with a personal mission—to get them home safely.

Did the chaplain's words find their mark? In the life of one man they did. After a battle one of the young soldiers was found dead, his right hand clutching the index finger of the left. "The LORD is my shepherd . . ."[2]

I pray that your final hours will find you clutching the same hope.

11

When Mourning Comes

The Burden of Grief

Though I walk through the valley of the shadow of death . . .

PSALM 23:4 NKJV

C arlos Andres Baisdon-Niño lay down with his favorite Bible storybook. He began with the first chapter and turned every page until the end. When he finished, he blew his good-night kisses to Mami and Papi, to his three *"niñas,"* and then, as always, he blew one to Papa Dios. He closed his eyes, drifted off to sleep, and awoke in heaven.

Carlos was three years old.

When Tim and Betsa, his parents, and I met to plan the funeral, they wanted me to watch a video of Carlos. "You've got to see him dancing," Tim told me. One look and I could see why. What little Carlos did to the rhythm of a Latin song can't be described with words. He shook from top to bottom. His feet moved, his hands bounced, his head swayed. You got the impression that his heart rate had switched over to his native Colombian beat.

We laughed, the three of us did. And in the laughter, for just a moment, Carlos was with us. For just a moment there was no leukemia, syringes, blankets, or chemotherapy. There was no stone to carve or grave to dig. There was just Carlos. And Carlos was just dancing.

But then the video stopped, and so did the laughter. And this mom and dad resumed their slow walk through the valley of the shadow of death.

Are you passing through the same shadow? Is this book being held by the same hands that touched the cold face of a friend? And the eyes that fall upon this page, have they also fallen upon the breathless figure of a husband, wife, or child? Are you passing through the valley? If not, this chapter may seem unnecessary. Feel free to move on—it will be here when you need it.

If so, however, you know that the black bag of sorrow is hard to bear.

It's hard to bear because not everyone understands your grief. They did at first. They did at the funeral. They did at the graveside. But they don't now; they don't understand. Grief lingers.

As silently as a cloud slides between you and the afternoon sun, memories drift between you and joy, leaving you in a chilly shadow. No warning. No notice. Just a whiff of the cologne he wore or a verse of the song she loved, and you are saying good-bye all over again.

Why won't the sorrow leave you alone?

Because you buried more than a person. You buried some of yourself. Wasn't it John Donne who said, "Any man's death diminishes me"? It's as if the human race resides on a huge trampoline. The movements of one can be felt by all. And the closer the relationship, the more profound the exit. When someone you love dies, it affects you.

It affects your dreams.

Some years ago my wife and I served with other missionaries in Rio de Janeiro, Brazil. Our team consisted of several young couples who, by virtue of being far away from home, became very close. We rejoiced greatly when two of our team members, Marty and Angela, announced that she was pregnant with their first child.

The pregnancy was difficult, however, and the joy became concern. Angela was told to stay in bed, and we were urged to stay in prayer. We did. And the Lord answered our prayers, though not as we desired. The baby died in the womb.

I've never forgotten Marty's comment. "More than a baby died, Max. A dream died."

Why does grief linger? Because you are dealing with more than memories—you are dealing with unlived tomorrows. You're not just battling sorrow—you're battling disappointment. You're also battling anger.

It may be on the surface. It may subterranean. It may be a flame. It may be a blowtorch. But anger lives in sorrow's house. Anger at self. Anger at life. Anger at the military or the hospital or the highway system. But most of all, anger at God. Anger that takes the form of the three-letter question—why? Why him? Why her? Why now? Why us?

You and I both know I can't answer that question. Only God knows the reasons behind his actions. But here is a key truth on which we can stand.

Our God is a good God.

"You are good, LORD. The LORD is good and right" (Ps. 25:7–8).

"Taste and see that the LORD is good" (Ps. 34:8 NIV).

God is a good God. We must begin here. Though we don't understand his actions, we can trust his heart.

God does only what is good. But how can death be good? Some mourners don't ask this question. When the quantity of years has outstripped the quality of years, we don't ask how death can be good.

But the father of the dead teenager does. The thirty-year-old widow does. The parents of Carlos did. My friends in Rio did. How could death be good?

Part of the answer may be found in Isaiah 57:1–2: "Good people are taken away, but no one understands. Those who do right are being taken away from evil and are given peace. Those who live as God wants find rest in death."

Death is God's way of taking people away from evil. From what kind of evil? An extended disease? An addiction? A dark season of rebellion? We don't know. But we know that no person lives one day more or less than God intends. "All the days planned for me were written in your book before I was one day old" (Ps. 139:16).

But her days here were so few . . .

His life was so brief . . .

To us it seems that way. We speak of a short life, but compared to eternity, who has a long one? A person's days on earth may appear as a drop in the ocean. Yours and mine may seem like a thimbleful. But compared to the Pacific of eternity, even the years of Methuselah filled no more than a glass. James was not speaking just to the young when he said, "Your life is like a mist. You can see it for a short time, but then it goes away" (James 4:14).

In God's plan every life is long enough and every death is timely. And though you and I might wish for a longer life, God knows better.

And—this is important—though you and I may wish a longer life for our loved ones, they don't. Ironically, the first to accept God's decision of death is the one who dies.

While we are shaking heads in disbelief, they are lifting hands in worship. While we are mourning at a grave, they are marveling at heaven. While we are questioning God, they are praising God.

But, Max, what of those who die with no faith? My husband never prayed. My grandpa never worshiped. My mother never opened a Bible, much less her heart. What about the one who never believed?

How do we know he didn't?

Who among us is privy to a person's final thoughts? Who among us knows what transpires in those final moments? Are you sure no prayer was offered? Eternity can bend the proudest knees. Could a person stare into the yawning canyon of death without whispering a plea for mercy? And could our God, who is partial to the humble, resist it?

He couldn't on Calvary. The confession of the thief on the cross was both a first and final one. But Christ heard it. Christ received it. Maybe you never heard your loved one confess Christ, but who's to say Christ didn't?

We don't know the final thoughts of a dying soul, but we know this. We know our God is a good God. He is "not willing that any should perish but that all should come to repentance" (2 Pet. 3:9 NKJV). He wants your loved one in heaven more than you do. And he usually gets what he wants.

You know what else God wants? He wants you to face your sorrow. Denial and dismissal are not a part of God's grief therapy.

David faced his. When he learned of the death of Saul and Jonathan, David and the entire army tore their clothing, wept aloud, and fasted until sunset. His lament was intense and public. "May there be no dew or rain on the mountains of Gilboa," he mourned, "and may their fields produce no grain. . . . We loved Saul and Jonathan and enjoyed them while they lived. They are together even in death. They were faster than eagles. They were stronger than lions" (2 Sam. 1:21–23).

David not only sang this dirge, he "ordered that the people of Judah be taught this song" (v. 18). Death was not soft-pedaled or passed over. Face it, fight it, question it, or condemn it, but don't deny it. As his son Solomon explained, "There is . . . a time to mourn" (Eccles. 3:1, 4 NIV). Don't heed, but do forgive, those who urge you not to.

God will lead you *through*, not around, the valley of the shadow of death. And, by the way, aren't you glad it's just a shadow?

Dr. Donald Grey Barnhouse told of the occasion of his first wife's death. He and his children were driving home from the burial, overcome with grief. He searched for a word of comfort to offer but could think of nothing. Just then, a large moving van drove by. As it passed, the shadow of the truck swept over the car. An inspiration came to Dr. Barnhouse. He turned to his family and asked, "Children, would you rather be run over by a truck or by its shadow?"

The children said, "Well, of course, Dad, we'd rather be run over by the shadow. That can't hurt us at all."

Dr. Barnhouse explained, "Did you know that two thousand years ago the truck of death ran over the Lord Jesus . . . in order that only its shadow might run over us?"[1]

We face death, but thanks to Jesus, we only face its shadow. And thanks to Jesus, we believe that our loved ones are happy and that the little Carloses of the world are dancing as never before.

12

From Panic to Peace

The Burden of Fear

I will fear no evil.

I t's the expression of Jesus that puzzles us. We've never seen his face like this.

Jesus smiling, yes.

Jesus weeping, absolutely.

Jesus stern, even that.

But Jesus anguished? Cheeks streaked with tears? Face flooded in sweat? Rivulets of blood dripping from his chin? You remember the night.

> Jesus left the city and went to the Mount of Olives, as he often did, and his followers went with him. When he reached the place, he said to them, "Pray for strength against temptation."
>
> Then Jesus went about a stone's throw away from them. He kneeled down and prayed, "Father, if you are willing, take away this cup of suffering. But do what you want, not what I want." Then an angel from heaven appeared to him to strengthen him. Being full of pain, Jesus prayed even harder. His sweat was like drops of blood falling to the ground. (Luke 22:39–44)

The Bible I carried as a child contained a picture of Jesus in the Garden of Gethsemane. His face was soft, hands calmly folded as he knelt beside a rock and prayed. Jesus seemed peaceful. One reading of the Gospels disrupts that image. Mark says, "Jesus fell to the ground" (Mark 14:35). Matthew tells us Jesus was "very sad and troubled . . . to the point of death" (Matt. 26:37–38). According to Luke, Jesus was "full of pain" (Luke 22:44).

Equipped with those passages, how would you paint this scene? Jesus flat on the ground? Face in the dirt? Extended hands gripping grass? Body rising and falling with sobs? Face as twisted as the olive trees that surround him?

What do we do with this image of Jesus?

Simple. We turn to it when we look the same. We read it when we feel the same; we read it when we feel afraid. For isn't it likely that fear is one of the emotions Jesus felt? One might even argue that fear was the primary emotion. He saw something in the future so fierce, so foreboding that he begged for a change of plans. "Father, if you are willing, take away this cup of suffering" (Luke 22:42).

What causes you to pray the same prayer? Boarding an airplane? Facing a crowd? Public speaking? Taking a job? Taking a spouse? Driving on a highway? The source of your fear may seem small to others. But to you, it freezes your feet, makes your heart pound, and brings blood to your face. That's what happened to Jesus.

He was so afraid that he bled. Doctors describe this condition as hematidrosis. Severe anxiety causes the release of chemicals that break down the capillaries in the sweat glands. When this occurs, sweat comes out tinged with blood.

Jesus was more than anxious; he was afraid. Fear is worry's big brother. If worry is a burlap bag, fear is a trunk of concrete. It wouldn't budge.

How remarkable that Jesus felt such fear. But how kind that he told us about it. We tend to do the opposite. Gloss over our fears. Cover them up. Keep our sweaty palms in our pockets, our nausea and dry mouths a secret. Not so with Jesus. We see no mask of strength. But we do hear a request for strength.

"Father, if you are willing, take away this cup of suffering." The first one to hear his fear is his Father. He could have gone to his mother. He could have confided in his disciples. He could have assembled a prayer meeting. All would have been appropriate, but none were his priority. He went first to his Father.

Oh, how we tend to go everywhere else. First to the bar, to the counselor, to the self-help book or the friend next door. Not Jesus. The first one to hear his fear was his Father in heaven.

A millennium earlier David was urging the fear-filled to do the same. "I will fear no evil." How could David make such a claim? Because he knew where to look. "You are with me; Your rod and Your staff, they comfort me."

Rather than turn to the other sheep, David turned to the Shepherd. Rather than stare at the problems, he stared at the rod and staff. Because he knew where to look, David was able to say, "I will fear no evil."

I know a fellow who has a fear of crowds. When encircled by large groups, his breath grows short, panic surfaces, and he begins to sweat like a sumo wrestler in a sauna. He received some help, curiously, from a golfing buddy.

The two were at a movie theatre, waiting their turn to enter, when fear struck again. The crowd closed in like a forest. He wanted out and out fast. His buddy told him to take a few deep breaths. Then he helped manage the crisis by reminding him of the golf course.

"When you are hitting your ball out of the rough, and you are surrounded by trees, what do you do?"

"I look for an opening."

"You don't stare at the trees?"

"Of course not. I find an opening and focus on hitting the ball through it."

"Do the same in the crowd. When you feel the panic, don't focus on the people; focus on the opening."

Good counsel in golf. Good counsel in life. Rather than focus on the fear, focus on the solution.

That's what Jesus did.

That's what David did.

And that's what the writer of Hebrews urges us to do. "Let us run with endurance the race that is set before us, looking unto Jesus, the author and finisher of our faith" (Heb. 12:1–2 NKJV).

The writer of Hebrews was not a golfer, but he could have been a jogger, for he speaks of a runner and a forerunner. The forerunner is Jesus, the "author and finisher of our faith." He is the author—that is to say he wrote the book on salvation. And he is the finisher—he not only charted the map, he blazed the trail. He is the forerunner, and we are the runners. And we runners are urged to keep our eyes on Jesus.

I'm a runner. More mornings than not I drag myself out of bed and onto the street. I don't run fast. And compared to marathoners, I don't run far. But I run. I run because I don't like cardiologists. Nothing personal, mind you. It's just that I come from a family that keeps them in business. One told my dad he needed to retire. Another opened the chests of both my mom and brother. I'd like to be the one family member who doesn't keep a heart surgeon's number on speed dial.

Since heart disease runs in our family, I run in our neighborhood. As the sun is rising, I am running. And as I am running, my body is groaning. It doesn't want to cooperate. My knee hurts. My hip is stiff. My ankles complain. Sometimes a passerby laughs at my legs, and my ego hurts.

Things hurt. And as things hurt, I've learned that I have three options. Go home. (Denalyn would laugh at me.) Meditate on my hurts until I start imagining I'm having chest pains. (Pleasant thought.) Or I can keep running and watch the sun come up. My trail has just enough easterly bend to give me a front-row seat for God's morning miracle. If I watch God's world go from dark to golden, guess what? The same happens to my attitude. The pain passes and the joints loosen, and before I know it, the run is half over and life ain't half bad. Everything improves as I fix my eyes on the sun.

Wasn't that the counsel of the Hebrew epistle—"looking unto Jesus"? What was the focus of David? "You are with me; Your rod and Your staff, they comfort me."

How did Jesus endure the terror of the crucifixion? He went first to the Father with his fears. He modeled the words of Psalm 56:3: "When I am afraid, I put my trust in you" (NLT).

Do the same with yours. Don't avoid life's Gardens of Gethsemane. Enter them. Just don't enter them alone. And while there, be honest. Pounding the ground is permitted. Tears are allowed. And if you sweat blood, you won't be the first. Do what Jesus did; open your heart.

And be specific. Jesus was. "Take *this* cup," he prayed. Give God the number of the flight. Tell him the length of the speech. Share the details of the job transfer. He has plenty of time. He also has plenty of compassion.

He doesn't think your fears are foolish or silly. He won't tell you to "buck up" or "get tough." He's been where you are. He knows how you feel.

And he knows what you need. That's why we punctuate our prayers as Jesus did. "If you are willing . . ."

Was God willing? Yes and no. He didn't take away the cross, but he took the fear. God didn't still the storm, but he calmed the sailor.

Who's to say he won't do the same for you?

"Do not be anxious about anything, but in everything, by prayer and petition, with thanksgiving, present your requests to God" (Phil. 4:6 NIV).

Don't measure the size of the mountain; talk to the One who can move it. Instead of carrying the world on your shoulders, talk to the One who holds the universe on his. Hope is a look away.

Now, what were you looking at?

13

Silent Nights and Solitary Days

The Burden of Loneliness

You are with me.

PSALM 23:4 NKJV

A friend of mine worked at a pharmacy while attending the University of Texas. Steve's primary job was to deliver supplies to nursing homes in the Austin area. An additional task, however, involved a short trip next door.

Every four days he shouldered a large jug of water and carried it fifty or so feet to a building behind the pharmacy. The customer was an older woman, perhaps in her seventies, who lived alone in a dark, sparse, and tarnished apartment. A single light bulb hung from the ceiling. The wallpaper was stained and peeling. The shades were drawn, and the room was shadowy. Steve would deliver the jug, receive the payment, thank the woman, and leave.

Over the weeks he grew puzzled by her purchase. He learned that the woman had no other source of water. She would rely on his delivery for four days of washing, bathing, and drinking. Odd choice. Municipal water was cheaper. The city would have charged her twelve to fifteen dollars a month; her expense at the pharmacy added up to fifty dollars a month. Why didn't she choose the less expensive source?

The answer was in the delivery system. Yes, the city water cost less. But the city sent only the water; they didn't send a person. She preferred to pay more and see a human being than pay less and see no one.

Could anyone be that lonely?

It seems that David was. Some of his psalms have the feel of a lone oak on a winter prairie.

He wrote:

> Turn to me and be gracious to me,
>> for I am lonely and afflicted. (Ps. 25:16 NIV)

> I'm tired of all this—so tired. My bed
>> has been floating forty days and nights
> On the flood of my tears.
>> My mattress is soaked, soggy with tears.
> The sockets of my eyes are black holes;
>> Nearly blind, I squint and grope. (Ps. 6:6–7 MSG)

David knew what it feels like to be lonely . . . betrayed.

> When they were sick, I dressed in black;
>> instead of eating, I prayed.
> My prayers were like lead in my gut,
>> like I'd lost my best friend, my brother.
> I paced, distraught as a motherless child,
>> hunched and heavyhearted.

> But when I was down
>> they threw a party!
> All the nameless riffraff of the town came
>> chanting insults about me.
> Like barbarians desecrating a shrine,
>> they destroyed my reputation.

YAHWEH, how long are you going

to stand there doing nothing? (Ps. 35:13–17 MSG)

David knew the feeling of loneliness.

He knew it in his family. He was one of eight sons of Jesse. But when Samuel the prophet asked to see Jesse's boys, David was overlooked. The prophet counted and asked if there wasn't another child somewhere. Jesse snapped his fingers as if he'd forgotten his keys. "I still have the youngest son. He is out taking care of the sheep" (1 Sam. 16:11).

Jesse's term for "youngest son" was not complimentary. He literally said, "I still have the runt." Some of you were the runt in your family. The runt is the one the others have to put up with and keep an eye on. And on this day the runt was left out. How would you feel if a family meeting was called and your name wasn't?

Things didn't improve when he changed households.

His inclusion in the royal family was King Saul's idea. His exclusion was Saul's idea as well. Had David not ducked, he would have been pinned to the wall by the spear of the jealous king. But David did duck, and David did run. For ten years he ran. Into the wilderness he ran. Sleeping in caves, surviving on wild animals. He was hated and hunted like a jackal.

David was no stranger to loneliness.

You aren't either. By now you've learned that you don't have to be alone to feel lonely. Two thousand years ago 250 million people populated the earth. Now there are more than 5 billion. If loneliness could be cured by the presence of people, then surely there would be less loneliness today. But loneliness lingers.

Very early in my ministry I offered this Sunday morning prayer: "Thank you, Lord, for all our friends. We have so many we can't spend time with them all." After the service a successful businessman corrected

me, "You may have more friends than you can see. Not me. I have none."
A person can be surrounded by a church and still be lonely.

Loneliness is not the absence of faces. It is the absence of intimacy.
Loneliness doesn't come from being alone; it comes from feeling
alone. Feeling as if you are

> facing death alone,
>> facing disease alone,
>>> facing the future alone.

Whether it strikes you in your bed at night or on your drive to the
hospital, in the silence of an empty house or the noise of a crowded
bar, loneliness is when you think, *I feel so alone. Does anyone care?*

Bags of loneliness show up everywhere. They litter the floors of
boardrooms and clubs. We drag them into parties and usually drag
them back out. You'll spot them near the desk of the overworker,
beside the table of the overeater, and on the nightstand of the one-
night stand. We'll try anything to unload our loneliness. This is one
bag we want to drop quickly.

But should we? Should we be so quick to drop it? Rather than turn
from loneliness, what if we turned toward it? Could it be that loneliness is not a curse but a gift? A gift from God?

Wait a minute, Max. That can't be. Loneliness heavies my heart.
Loneliness leaves me empty and depressed. Loneliness is anything but
a gift.

You may be right, but work with me for a moment. I wonder if
loneliness is God's way of getting our attention.

Here's what I mean. Suppose you borrow a friend's car. His radio
doesn't work, but his CD player does. You rummage through his collec-
tion, looking for your style of music—let's say, country-western. But you
find nothing. He has nothing but his style of music—let's say, classical.

It's a long trip. And you can talk to yourself for only so long. So eventually you reach for a CD. You'd prefer some steel guitar, but you're stuck with soaring tenors. Initially it's tolerable. At least it fills the air. But eventually it's enjoyable. Your heart picks up the pattern of the kettledrums, your head rolls with the cellos, and you even catch yourself attempting a little Italian aria. "Hey, this isn't so bad."

Now, let me ask you. Would you have made this discovery on your own? No. What led to it? What caused you to hear music you'd never heard before? Simple. You had no other choice, no other option. You had nowhere else to go. Finally, when the silence was too loud, you took a chance on a song you'd never heard.

Oh, how God wants you to hear his music.

He has a rhythm that will race your heart and lyrics that will stir your tears. You want to journey to the stars? He can take you there. You want to lie down in peace? His music can soothe your soul.

But first, he's got to get rid of that country-western stuff. (Forgive me, Nashville. Only an example.)

And so he begins tossing the CDs. A friend turns away. The job goes bad. Your spouse doesn't understand. The church is dull. One by one he removes the options until all you have left is God.

He would do that? Absolutely. "The Lord disciplines those he loves" (Heb. 12:6). If he must silence every voice, he will. He wants you to hear his music. He wants you to discover what David discovered and to be able to say what David said.

"You are with me."

Yes, you, Lord, are in heaven. Yes, you rule the universe. Yes, you sit upon the stars and make your home in the deep. But yes, yes, yes, you are with me.

The Lord is with me. The Creator is with me. Yahweh is with me.

Moses proclaimed it: "What great nation has a god as near to them as the LORD our God is near to us" (Deut. 4:7 NLT).

Paul announced it: "He is not far from each one of us" (Acts 17:27 NIV).

And David discovered it: "You are with me."

Somewhere in the pasture, wilderness, or palace, David discovered that God meant business when he said:

"I will not leave you" (Gen. 28:15).

"I will . . . not forsake My people" (1 Kings 6:13 NKJV).

"The LORD will not abandon His people" (Ps. 94:14 NASB).

"God . . . will never leave you nor forsake you" (Deut. 31:6 NIV).

The discovery of David is indeed the message of Scripture—*the Lord is with us*. And, since the Lord is near, everything is different. Everything!

You may be facing death, but you aren't facing death alone; the Lord is with you. You may be facing unemployment, but you aren't facing unemployment alone; the Lord is with you. You may be facing marital struggles, but you aren't facing them alone; the Lord is with you. You may be facing debt, but you aren't facing debt alone; the Lord is with you.

Underline these words: You are not alone.

Your family may turn against you, but God won't. Your friends may betray you, but God won't. You may feel alone in the wilderness, but you are not. He is with you. And because he is, everything is different. *You* are different.

God changes your *n* into a *v*. You go from *lonely* to *lovely*.

When you know God loves you, you won't be desperate for the love of others.

You'll no longer be a hungry shopper at the market. Have you ever gone to the grocery on an empty stomach? You're a sitting duck. You buy everything you don't need. Doesn't matter if it is good for you— you just want to fill your tummy. When you're lonely, you do the same in life, pulling stuff off the shelf, not because you need it, but because you are hungry for love.

Why do we do it? Because we fear facing life alone. For fear of not fitting in, we take the drugs. For fear of standing out, we wear the clothes. For fear of appearing small, we go into debt and buy the house. For fear of going unnoticed, we dress to seduce or to impress. For fear of sleeping alone, we sleep with anyone. For fear of not being loved, we search for love in all the wrong places.

But all that changes when we discover God's perfect love. And "perfect love casts out fear" (1 John 4:18 NKJV).

Loneliness. Could it be one of God's finest gifts? If a season of solitude is his way to teach you to hear his song, don't you think it's worth it?

So do I.

14

The Crowing Rooster and Me

The Burden of Shame

You prepare a table before me in the presence of my enemies.

PSALM 23:5 NKJV

S ee the fellow in the shadows? That's Peter. Peter the apostle. Peter the impetuous. Peter the passionate. He once walked on water. Stepped right out of the boat onto the lake. He'll soon preach to thousands. Fearless before friends and foes alike. But tonight the one who stepped on the water has hurried into hiding. The one who will speak with power is weeping in pain.

Not sniffling or whimpering, but weeping. Bawling. Bearded face buried in thick hands. His howl echoing in the Jerusalem night. What hurts more? The fact that he did it? Or the fact that he swore he never would?

"Lord, I am ready to go with you to prison and even to die with you!" he pledged only hours earlier. "But Jesus said, 'Peter, before the rooster crows this day, you will say three times that you don't know me'" (Luke 22:33–34).

Denying Christ on the night of his betrayal was bad enough, but did he have to boast that he wouldn't? And one denial was pitiful, but three? Three denials were horrific, but did he have to curse? "Peter began to place a curse on himself and swear, 'I don't know the man'" (Matt. 26:74).

And now, awash in a whirlpool of sorrow, Peter is hiding. Peter is weeping. And soon Peter will be fishing.

We wonder why he goes fishing. We know why he goes to Galilee.

He had been told that the risen Christ would meet the disciples there. The arranged meeting place is not the sea, however, but a mountain (Matt. 28:16). If the followers were to meet Jesus on a mountain, what are they doing in a boat? No one told them to fish, but that's what they did. "Simon Peter said, 'I am going out to fish.' The others said, 'We will go with you'" (John 21:3). Besides, didn't Peter quit fishing? Two years earlier, when Jesus called him to fish for men, didn't he drop his net and follow? We haven't seen him fish since. We never see him fish again. Why is he fishing now? Especially now! Jesus has risen from the dead. Peter has seen the empty tomb. Who could fish at a time like this?

Were they hungry? Perhaps that's the sum of it. Maybe the expedition was born out of growling stomachs.

Or then again, maybe it was born out of a broken heart.

You see, Peter could not deny his denial. The empty tomb did not erase the crowing rooster. Christ had returned, but Peter wondered, he must have wondered, "After what I did, would he return for someone like me?"

We've wondered the same. Is Peter the only person to do the very thing he swore he'd never do?

"Infidelity is behind me!"

"From now on, I'm going to bridle my tongue."

"No more shady deals. I've learned my lesson."

Oh, the volume of our boasting. And, oh, the heartbreak of our shame.

Rather than resist the flirting, we return it.

Rather than ignore the gossip, we share it.

Rather than stick to the truth, we shade it.

And the rooster crows, and conviction pierces, and Peter has a partner in the shadows. We weep as Peter wept, and we do what Peter did. We go fishing. We go back to our old lives. We return to our pre-Jesus practices. We do what comes naturally, rather than what comes spiritually. And we question whether Jesus has a place for folks like us.

Jesus answers that question. He answers it for you and me and all who tend to "Peter out" on Christ. His answer came on the shore of the sea in a gift to Peter. You know what Jesus did? Split the waters? Turn the boat to gold and the nets to silver? No, Jesus did something much more meaningful. He invited Peter to breakfast. Jesus prepared a meal.

Of course, the breakfast was one special moment among several that morning. There was the great catch of fish and the recognition of Jesus. The plunge of Peter and the paddling of the disciples. And there was the moment they reached the shore and found Jesus next to a fire of coals. The fish were sizzling, and the bread was waiting, and the defeater of hell and the ruler of heaven invited his friends to sit down and have a bite to eat.

No one could have been more grateful than Peter. The one Satan had sifted like wheat was eating bread at the hand of God. Peter was welcomed to the meal of Christ. Right there for the devil and his tempters to see, Jesus "prepared a table in the presence of his enemies."

OK, so maybe Peter didn't say it that way. But David did. "You prepare a table before me in the presence of my enemies" (Ps. 23:5 NKJV). What the shepherd did for the sheep sounds a lot like what Jesus did for Peter.

At this point in the psalm, David's mind seems to be lingering in the high country with the sheep. Having guided the flock through the valley to the alp lands for greener grass, he remembers the shepherd's added responsibility. He must prepare the pasture.

This is new land, so the shepherd must be careful. Ideally, the grazing area will be flat, a mesa or tableland. The shepherd searches for poisonous plants and ample water. He looks for signs of wolves, coyotes, and bears.

Of special concern to the shepherd is the adder, a small brown snake that lives underground. Adders are known to pop out of their holes and nip the sheep on the nose. The bite often infects and can even kill. As defense against the snake, the shepherd pours a circle of oil at the top of each adder's hole. He also applies the oil to the noses of the animals. The oil on the snake's hole lubricates the exit, preventing the snake from climbing out. The smell of the oil on the sheep's nose drives the serpent away. The shepherd, in a very real sense, has prepared the table.[1]

What if your Shepherd did for you what the shepherd did for his flock? Suppose he dealt with your enemy, the devil, and prepared for you a safe place of nourishment? What if Jesus did for you what he did for Peter? Suppose he, in the hour of your failure, invited you to a meal?

What would you say if I told you he has done exactly that?

On the night before his death, Jesus prepared a table for his followers.

On the first day of the Festival of Unleavened Bread, the day the lambs for the Passover meal were killed, Jesus' disciples asked him, "Where do you want us to go and get the Passover meal ready for you?"

Then Jesus sent two of them with these instructions: "Go into the city, and a man carrying a jar of water will meet you. Follow him to the house he enters, and say to the owner of the house: 'The Teacher says, Where is the room where my disciples and I will eat the Passover meal?' Then he will show you a large, upstairs room, fixed up and furnished, where you will get everything ready for us." (Mark 14:12–15 TEV)

Look who did the "preparing" here. Jesus reserved a large room and arranged for the guide to lead the disciples. Jesus made certain the room was furnished and the food set out. What did the disciples do? They faithfully complied and were fed.

The Shepherd prepared the table.

Not only that, he dealt with the snakes. You'll remember that only one of the disciples didn't complete the meal that night. "The devil had already persuaded Judas Iscariot, the son of Simon, to turn against Jesus" (John 13:2). Judas started to eat, but Jesus didn't let him finish. On the command of Jesus, Judas left the room. "'The thing that you will do—do it quickly.' . . . Judas took the bread Jesus gave him and immediately went out. It was night" (John 13:27, 30).

There is something dynamic in this dismissal. Jesus prepared a table in the presence of the enemy. Judas was allowed to see the supper, but he wasn't allowed to stay there.

You are not welcome here. This table is for my children. You may tempt them. You may trip them. But you will never sit with them. This is how much he loves us.

And if any doubt remains, lest there be any "Peters" who wonder if there is a place at the table for them, Jesus issues a tender reminder as he passes the cup. "Every one of you drink this. This is my blood which is the new agreement that God makes with his people. This blood is poured out for many to forgive their sins" (Matt. 26:27–28).

"*Every one* of you drink this." Those who feel unworthy, drink this. Those who feel ashamed, drink this. Those who feel embarrassed, drink this.

May I share a time when I felt all three?

By the age of eighteen I was well on my way to a drinking problem. My system had become so resistant to alcohol that a six-pack of beer had little or no impact on me. At the age of twenty, God not only saved me from hell after this life, he saved me from hell during it. Only he knows where I was headed, but I have a pretty good idea.

For that reason, part of my decision to follow Christ included no more beer. So I quit. But, curiously, the thirst for beer never left. It hasn't hounded me or consumed me, but two or three times a week the thought of a good beer sure entices me. Proof to me that I have to be careful is this—nonalcoholic beers have no appeal. It's not the flavor of the drink; it's the buzz. But for more than twenty years, drinking has never been a major issue.

A couple of years ago, however, it nearly became one. I lowered my guard a bit. *One beer with barbecue won't hurt.* Then another time with Mexican food. Then a time or two with no food at all. Over a period of two months I went from no beers to maybe one or two a week. Again, for most people, no problem, but for me it could become one.

You know when I began to smell trouble? One hot Friday afternoon I was on my way to speak at our annual men's retreat. Did I say the day was hot? Brutally hot. I was thirsty. Soda wouldn't do. So I began to plot. Where could I buy a beer and not be seen by anyone I knew?

With that thought, I crossed a line. What's done in secret is best not done at all. But I did it anyway. I drove to an out-of-the-way convenience store, parked, and waited until all patrons had left. I entered, bought my beer, held it close to my side, and hurried to the car.

That's when the rooster crowed.

It crowed because I was sneaking around. It crowed because I knew better. It crowed because, and this really hurt, the night before I'd scolded one of my daughters for keeping secrets from me. And now, what was I doing?

I threw the beer in the trash and asked God to forgive me. A few days later I shared my struggle with the elders and some members of the congregation and was happy to chalk up the matter to experience and move on.

But I couldn't. The shame plagued me. Of all the people to do such a thing. So many could be hurt by my stupidity. And of all the times to do such a thing. En route to minister at a retreat. What hypocrisy!

I felt like a bum. Forgiveness found its way into my head, but the elevator designed to lower it eighteen inches to my heart was out of order.

And, to make matters worse, Sunday rolled around. I found myself on the front row of the church, awaiting my turn to speak. Again, I had been honest with God, honest with the elders, honest with myself. But still, I struggled. Would God want a guy like me to preach?

The answer came in the Supper. The Lord's Supper. The same Jesus who'd prepared a meal for Peter had prepared one for me. The same Shepherd who had trumped the devil trumped him again. The same Savior who had built a fire on the shore stirred a few embers in my heart.

"Every one of you drink this." And so I did. It felt good to be back at the table.

15

Slippery Sheep and Healed Hurts

The Burden of Disappointment

You anoint my head with oil.

PSALM 23:5 NKJV

D *is* changes everything. With *dis,* "obey" becomes *"dis*obey." "Respect" is changed to *"dis*respect." "Regard" is suddenly *"dis*regard." What was an "ability" becomes a *"dis*ability." "Engage" is now *"dis*engage," and "grace" is transformed into *"disgrace."* All because of *dis.*

We'd be hard pressed to find a more potent trio of letters. And we'd be hard pressed to find a better example of their power than the word *appointment.*

Most of us like appointments. Even the organizationally inept like appointments. Appointments create a sense of predictability in an unpredictable world. Down deep we know we control the future as much as a caboose controls the train, yet our Day-Timers give us the illusion that we do.

A disappointment reminds us that we don't. A disappointment is a missed appointment. What we hoped would happen, didn't. We wanted health; we got disease. We wanted retirement; we got reassignment. Divorce instead of family. Dismissal instead of promotion. Now what? What do we do with our disappointments?

We could do what Miss Haversham did. Remember her in Charles Dickens's *Great Expectations?* Jilted by her fiancé just prior to the wedding, her appointment became a missed appointment and a disappointment. How did she respond? Not too well. She closed all the blinds in the house, stopped every clock, left the wedding cake on the table to gather cobwebs, and continued to wear her wedding dress until it hung in yellow decay around her shrunken form. Her wounded heart consumed her life.

We can follow the same course.

Or we can follow the example of the apostle Paul. His goal was to be a missionary in Spain. Rather than send Paul to Spain, however, God sent him to prison. Sitting in a Roman jail, Paul could have made the same choice as Miss Haversham, but he didn't. Instead he said, "As long as I'm here, I might as well write a few letters." Hence your Bible has the Epistles to Philemon, the Philippians, the Colossians, and the Ephesians.[1] No doubt Paul would have done a great work in Spain. But would it have compared with the work of those four letters?

You've sat where Paul sat. I know you have. You were hotter than a two-dollar pistol on the trail to Spain or college or marriage or independence . . . but then came the layoff or the pregnancy or the sick parent. And you ended up in prison. So long, Spain. Hello, Rome. So long, appointment. Hello, disappointment. Hello, pain.

How did you handle it? Better asked, how are you handling it? Could you use some help? I've got just what you need. Six words in the fifth verse of the Twenty-third Psalm: "You anoint my head with oil."

Don't see the connection? What does a verse on oil have to do with the hurt that come from the disappointments of life?

A little livestock lesson might help. In ancient Israel shepherds used oil for three purposes: to repel insects, to prevent conflicts, and to heal wounds.

Bugs bug people, but they can kill sheep. Flies, mosquitoes, and gnats can turn the summer into a time of torture for the livestock. Consider nose flies, for example. If they succeed in depositing their eggs into the soft membrane of the sheep's nose, the eggs become wormlike larvae, which drive the sheep insane. One shepherd explains: "For relief from this agonizing annoyance sheep will deliberately beat their heads against trees, rocks, posts, or brush. . . . In extreme cases of intense infestation a sheep may even kill itself in a frenzied endeavor to gain respite from the aggravation."[2]

When a swarm of nose flies appears, sheep panic. They run. They hide. They toss their heads up and down for hours. They forget to eat. They aren't able to sleep. Ewes stop milking, and lambs stop growing. The entire flock can be disrupted, even destroyed by the presence of a few flies.

For this reason, the shepherd anoints the sheep. He covers their heads with an oil-like repellent. The fragrance keeps the insects at bay and the flock at peace.

At peace, that is, until mating season. Most of the year, sheep are calm, passive animals. But during mating season, everything changes. The rams put the "ram" in *rambunctious*. They strut around the pasture and flex their necks, trying to win the attention of the new gal on the block. When a ram catches her eye, he tosses his head back and says, "I want ewe, baby." About that time her boyfriend shows up and tells her to go someplace safe. "Ewe better move, sweetie. This could get ugly." The two rams lower their heads and POW! An old-fashioned head butt breaks out.

To prevent injury, the shepherd anoints the rams. He smears a slippery, greasy substance over the nose and head. This lubricant causes them to glance off rather than crash into each other.

They still tend to get hurt, however. And these wounds are the third reason the shepherd anoints the sheep.

Most of the wounds the shepherd treats are simply the result of living in a pasture. Thorns prick or rocks cut or a sheep rubs its head too hard against a tree. Sheep get hurt. As a result, the shepherd regularly, often daily, inspects the sheep, searching for cuts and abrasions. He doesn't want the cut to worsen. He doesn't want today's wound to become tomorrow's infection.

Neither does God. Just like sheep, we have wounds, but ours are wounds of the heart that come from disappointment after disappointment. If we're not careful, these wounds lead to bitterness. And so just like sheep, we need to be treated. "He made us, and we belong to him; we are his people, the sheep he tends" (Ps. 100:3).

Sheep aren't the only ones who need preventive care, and sheep aren't the only ones who need a healing touch. We also get irritated with each other, butt heads, and then get wounded. Many of our disappointments in life begin as irritations. The large portion of our problems are not lion-sized attacks, but rather the day-to-day swarm of frustrations and mishaps and heartaches. You don't get invited to the dinner party. You don't make the team. You don't get the scholarship. Your boss doesn't notice your hard work. Your husband doesn't notice your new dress. Your neighbor doesn't notice the mess in his yard. You find yourself more irritable, more gloomy, more . . . well, more hurt.

Like the sheep, you don't sleep well, you don't eat well. You may even hit your head against a tree a few times.

Or you may hit your head against a person. It's amazing how hard-headed we can be with each other. Some of our deepest hurts come from butting heads with people.

Like the sheep, the rest of our wounds come just from living in the pasture. The pasture of the sheep, however, is much more appealing. The sheep have to face wounds from thorns and thistles. We have to face aging, loss, and illness. Some of us face betrayal and injustice. Live long enough in this world, and most of us will face deep, deep hurts of some kind or another.

So we, like the sheep, get wounded. And we, like the sheep, have a shepherd. Remember the words we read? "We belong to him; we are his people, the sheep he tends" (Ps. 100:3). He will do for you what the shepherd does for the sheep. He will tend to you.

If the Gospels teach us anything, they teach us that Jesus is a Good Shepherd. "I am the good shepherd," Jesus announces. "The good shepherd gives his life for the sheep" (John 10:11).

Didn't Jesus spread the oil of prevention on his disciples? He prayed for them. He equipped them before he sent them out. He revealed to them the secrets of the parables. He interrupted their arguments and calmed their fears. Because he was a good shepherd, he protected them against disappointments.

Not only did Jesus prevent wounds, he healed them. He touched the eyes of the blind man. He touched the disease of the leper. He touched the body of the dead girl. Jesus tends to his sheep. He touched the searching heart of Nicodemus. He touched the open heart of Zacchaeus. He touched the broken heart of Mary Magdalene. He touched the confused heart of Cleopas. And he touched the stubborn heart of Paul and the repentant heart of Peter. Jesus tends to his sheep. And he will tend to you.

If you will let him. How? How do you let him? The steps are so simple.

First, go to him. David would trust his wounds to no other person but God. He said, "*You* anoint my head with oil." Not, "your prophets," "your teachers," or "your counselors." Others may guide us to God. Others may help us understand God. But no one does the work of God, for only God can heal. God "heals the brokenhearted" (Ps. 147:3).

Have you taken your disappointments to God? You've shared them with your neighbor, your relatives, your friends. But have you taken them to God? James says, "Anyone who is having troubles should pray" (James 5:13).

Before you go anywhere else with your disappointments, go to God.

Maybe you don't want to trouble God with your hurts. *After all, he's got famines and pestilence and wars; he won't care about my little struggles,* you think. Why don't you let him decide that? He cared enough about a wedding to provide the wine. He cared enough about Peter's tax payment to give him a coin. He cared enough about the woman at the well to give her answers. "He cares about you" (1 Pet. 5:7).

Your first step is to go to the right person. Go to God. Your second step is to assume the right posture. Bow before God.

In order to be anointed, the sheep must stand still, lower their heads, and let the shepherd do his work. Peter urges us to "be humble under God's powerful hand so he will lift you up when the right time comes" (1 Pet. 5:6).

When we come to God, we make requests; we don't make demands. We come with high hopes and a humble heart. We state what we want, but we pray for what is right. And if God gives us the prison of Rome instead of the mission of Spain, we accept it because we know "God will always give what is right to his people who cry to him night and day, and he will not be slow to answer them" (Luke 18:7).

We go to him. We bow before him, and we *trust in him.*

The sheep doesn't understand why the oil repels the flies. The sheep doesn't understand how the oil heals the wounds. In fact, all the sheep knows is that something happens in the presence of the shepherd. And that's all we need to know as well. "LORD, I give myself to you; my God, I trust you" (Ps. 25:1–2).

Go.

Bow.

Trust.

Worth a try, don't you think?

16

Jam Session

The Burden of Envy

My cup overflows with blessings.

A member of our church gave me a jar of homemade peach preserves a couple of weeks ago. Few delicacies in life compare with her peach preserves. Should I someday face a firing squad, I'll pass on the cigarette but be the first to perk up if Sarah's peach preserves are offered. Each spoonful is a celestial experience. The only problem with her gift was that it didn't last. I'm sad to report that the bottom of my jar is in sight. I'll soon be shaking out the last drop like a lost cowboy shakes his canteen.

To be quite honest, I'm dreading the moment. Its proximity has affected my behavior. Anyone who requests a taste of my peach preserves is met with a Clint Eastwood snarl, "Don't even think about it."

If I were Sarah's husband, Keith, I wouldn't have such a problem. He gets all the peach preserves he wants. Does the clinking of the spoon at the bottom of the jar trigger tears for Keith? Hardly, he has an unlimited supply. One might even say that he has more than he deserves. And one might wonder why he has so much and I have so little. Why should he have a pantryful and I just a jarful? Who gave him the key to the jam-and-jelly castle? Who made him the master of marmalades? Who crowned Keith the king of confitures? It's not fair. It's not right. In fact, the more I think about it . . .

Which is exactly what I shouldn't do. I shouldn't think about it. For resting at the end of this trail of thought is the deadly briefcase of envy.

If you haven't seen one in real life, you've seen one in the spy movies. The assassin carries it up the back stairs into the vacated room at the top of the building. When he is sure no one can see him, he opens the case. The disassembled rifle sits in cushioned slots. The scope, the barrel, the stock—all await the hand of the marksman. The marksman awaits the arrival of his victim.

Who is his victim? Anyone who has more than he has. More karats, more horsepower, more office space, more church members. Jealousy sets her cross hairs on the one who has more. "You want something you don't have, and you will do anything to get it. You will even kill!" (James 4:2 CEV).

Honestly, Max, I would never do that. I would never kill.

With a rifle, maybe not. But with your tongue? With your glare? Your gossip? "Jealousy," informs Proverbs 6:34, "enrages a man" (NASB). Are your sights set on someone? If so, be careful; "jealousy will rot your bones" (Prov. 14:30).

Need a deterrent for envy? An antidote for jealousy? The psalm we are studying offers one. Rather than bemoan the peach preserves you don't have, rejoice in the abundant cup you do. "My cup overflows with blessings" (Ps. 23:5 NLT).

Is an overflowing cup full? Absolutely. The wine reaches the rim and then tumbles over the edge. The goblet is not large enough to contain the quantity. According to David, our hearts are not large enough to contain the blessings that God wants to give. He pours and pours until they literally flow over the edge and down on the table. You'll like the paragraph penned a century ago by F. B. Meyer:

> Whatever the blessing is in our cup, it is sure to run over. With him the calf is always the fatted calf; the robe is always the best robe; the joy is unspeakable; the peace passeth understanding. . . . There is no

grudging in God's benevolence; He does not measure out his goodness as an apothecary counts his drops and measures his drams,
slowly and exactly, drop by drop. God's way is always characterized by
multitudinous and overflowing bounty.[1]

The last thing we need to worry about is not having enough. Our
cup overflows with blessings.

Let me ask a question—a crucial question. If focusing on our diminishing items leads to envy, what would happen if we focused on the
unending items? If awareness of what we don't have creates jealousy,
is it possible that an awareness of our abundance will lead to contentment? Let's give it a try and see what happens. Let's dedicate a few
paragraphs to a couple of blessings that, according to the Bible, are
overflowing in our lives.

Abounding grace. "The more we see our sinfulness, the more we see
God's *abounding grace* forgiving us" (Rom. 5:20 TLB, emphasis mine).
To abound is to have a surplus, an abundance, an extravagant portion. Should the fish in the Pacific worry that it will run out of
ocean? No. Why? The ocean abounds with water. Need the lark be
anxious about finding room in the sky to fly? No. The sky abounds
with space.

Should the Christian worry that the cup of mercy will run empty?
He may. For he may not be aware of God's abounding grace. Are you?
Are you aware that the cup God gives you *overflows* with mercy? Or are
you afraid your cup will run dry? Your warranty will expire? Are you
afraid your mistakes are too great for God's grace?

We can't help but wonder if the apostle Paul had the same fear.
Before he was Paul the apostle, he was Saul the murderer. Before he
encouraged Christians, he murdered Christians. What would it be like
to live with such a past? Did he ever meet children whom he had made

orphans? Did their faces haunt his sleep? Did Paul ever ask, "Can God forgive a man like me?"

The answer to his and our questions is found in a letter he wrote to Timothy: "The grace of our Lord was poured out on me abundantly, along with the faith and love that are in Christ Jesus" (1 Tim. 1:14 NIV).

God is not a miser with his grace. Your cup may be low on cash or clout, but it is overflowing with mercy. You may not have the prime parking place, but you have sufficient pardon. "He will abundantly pardon" (Isa. 55:7 NKJV). Your cup overflows with grace.

Hope. And because it does, your cup overflows with hope. "God will help you overflow with hope in him through the Holy Spirit's power within you" (Rom. 15:13 TLB).

Heaven's hope does for your world what the sunlight did for my grandmother's cellar. I owe my love of peach preserves to her. She canned her own and stored them in an underground cellar near her West Texas house. It was a deep hole with wooden steps, plywood walls, and a musty smell. As a youngster I used to climb in, close the door, and see how long I could last in the darkness. Not even a slit of light entered that underground hole. I would sit silently, listening to my breath and heartbeats, until I couldn't take it anymore and then would race up the stairs and throw open the door. Light would avalanche into the cellar. What a change! Moments before I couldn't see anything—all of a sudden I could see everything.

Just as light poured into the cellar, God's hope pours into your world. Upon the sick, he shines the ray of healing. To the bereaved, he gives the promise of reunion. For the dying, he lit the flame of resurrection. To the confused, he offers the light of Scripture.

God gives hope. So what if someone was born thinner or stronger, lighter or darker than you? Why count diplomas or compare résumés?

What does it matter if they have a place at the head table? You have a place at God's table. And he is filling your cup to overflowing.

The overflowing cup was a powerful symbol in the days of David. Hosts in the ancient East used it to send a message to the guest. As long as the cup was kept full, the guest knew he was welcome. But when the cup sat empty, the host was hinting that the hour was late. On those occasions, however, when the host really enjoyed the company of the person, he filled the cup to overflowing. He didn't stop when the wine reached the rim; he kept pouring until the liquid ran over the edge of the cup and down on the table.[2]

Have you noticed how wet your table is? God wants you to stay. Your cup overflows with joy. Overflows with grace. Shouldn't your heart overflow with gratitude?

The heart of the boy did. Not at first, mind you. Initially he was full of envy. But, in time, he was full of gratitude.

According to the fable, he lived with his father in a valley at the base of a large dam. Every day the father would go to work on the mountain behind their house and return home with a wheelbarrow full of dirt. "Pour the dirt in the sacks, Son," the father would say. "And stack them in front of the house."

And though the boy would obey, he also complained. He was tired of dirt. He was weary of bags. Why didn't his father give him what other fathers gave their sons? They had toys and games; he had dirt. When he saw what the others had, he grew mad at them. "It's not fair," he said to himself.

And when he saw his father, he objected. "They have fun. I have dirt."

The father would smile and place his arm on the boy's shoulders and say, "Trust me, Son. I'm doing what is best."

But it was so hard for the boy to trust. Every day the father would bring the load. Every day the boy would fill bags. "Stack them as high as you can," the father would say as he went for more. And so the boy filled the bags and piled them high. So high he couldn't see over them.

"Work hard, Son," the father said one day. "We're running out of time." As the father spoke, he looked at the darkening sky. The boy stared at the clouds and turned to ask about them, but when he did, the thunder cracked and the sky opened. The rain poured so hard he could scarcely see his father through the water. "Keep stacking, Son!" And as he did, the boy heard a mighty crash.

The water of the river poured through the dam and toward the little village. In a moment the tide swept everything in its path, but the dike of dirt gave the boy and the father the time they needed. "Hurry, Son. Follow me."

They ran to the side of the mountain behind their house and into a tunnel. In a matter of moments they exited the other side and scampered up the hill and came upon a new cottage.

"We'll be safe here," the father said to the boy.

Only then did the son realize what the father had done. He had burrowed an exit. Rather than give him what he wanted, the father gave his boy what he needed. He gave him a safe passage and a safe place.

Hasn't our Father given us the same? A strong wall of grace to protect us? A sure exit to deliver us? Of whom can we be envious? Who has more than we do? Rather than want what others have, shouldn't we wonder if they have what we do? Instead of being jealous of them, how about zealous for them? For heaven's sake, drop the rifles and hold out the cup. There is enough to go around.

One thing is certain. When the final storm comes and you are safe in your Father's house, you won't regret what he didn't give. You'll be stunned at what he did.

God's Loving Pursuit

The Burden of Doubt

Surely goodness and mercy shall follow me
all the days of my life.

PSALM 23:6 NKJV

E ric Hill had everything you'd need for a bright future. He was twenty-eight years old and a recent college grad with an athletic frame and a soft smile. His family loved him, girls took notice of him, and companies had contacted him about working for them. Although Eric appeared composed without, he was tormented within. Tormented by voices he could not still. Bothered by images he could not avoid. So, hoping to get away from them all, he got away from it all. On a gray rainy day in February 1982, Eric Hill walked out the back door of his Florida home and never came back.

His sister Debbie remembers seeing him leave, his tall frame ambling down the interstate. She assumed he would return. He didn't. She hoped he would call. He didn't. She thought she could find him. She couldn't. Where Eric journeyed, only God and Eric know, and neither of them has chosen to tell. What we do know is Eric heard a voice. And in that voice was an "assignment." And that assignment was to pick up garbage along a roadside in San Antonio, Texas.

To the commuters on Interstate 10, his lanky form and bearded face became a familiar sight. He made a home out of a hole in a vacant lot. He made a wardrobe out of split trousers and a torn sweatshirt. An old hat deferred the summer sun. A plastic bag on his shoulders softened the winter chill. His weathered skin and stooped shoulders made him look twice his forty-four years. But then, sixteen years on the side of the road would do that to you.

That's how long it had been since Debbie had seen her brother. She might never have seen him again had it not been for two events. The first was the construction of a car dealership on Eric's vacant lot. The second was a severe pain in his abdomen. The dealership took his home. The pain nearly took his life.

EMS found him curled in a ball on the side of the road, clutching his stomach. The hospital ran some tests and found that Eric had cancer. Terminal cancer. Another few months and he would be dead. And with no known family or relatives, he would die alone.

His court-appointed attorney couldn't handle this thought. "Surely someone is looking for Eric," he reasoned. So the lawyer scoured the Internet for anyone in search of a brown-haired, adult male with the last name Hill. That's how he met Debbie.

His description seemed to match her memory, but she had to know for sure.

So Debbie came to Texas. She and her husband and two children rented a hotel room and set out to find Eric. By now he'd been released from the hospital, but the chaplain knew where he was. They found him sitting against a building not far from the interstate. As they approached, he stood. They offered fruit; he refused. They offered juice; he declined. He was polite but unimpressed with this family who claimed to be his own.

His interest perked, however, when Debbie offered him a pin to wear, an angel pin. He said yes. Her first time to touch her brother in sixteen years was the moment she allowed her to pin the angel on his shirt.

Debbie intended to spend a week. But a week passed, and she stayed. Her husband returned home, and she stayed. Spring became summer, and Eric improved, and still she stayed. Debbie rented an apartment and began homeschooling her kids and reaching out to her brother.

It wasn't easy. He didn't recognize her. He didn't know her. One day he cursed her. He didn't want to sleep in her apartment. He didn't want her food. He didn't want to talk. He wanted his vacant lot. He wanted his "job." Who was this woman anyway?

But Debbie didn't give up on Eric. She understood that he didn't understand. So she stayed.

I met her one Sunday when she visited our congregation. When she shared her story, I asked what you might want to ask "How do you keep from giving up?"

"Simple," she said. "He's my brother."

I told her that her pursuit reminded me of another pursuit—that her heart reminded me of another heart. Another kind heart who left home in search of the confused. Another compassionate soul who couldn't bear the thought of a brother or sister in pain. So, like Debbie, he left home. Like Debbie, he found his sibling.

And when Jesus found us, we acted like Eric. Our limitations kept us from recognizing the One who came to save us. We even doubted his presence—and sometimes we still do.

How does he deal with our doubts? He follows us. As Debbie followed Eric, God follows us. He pursues us until we finally see him as our Father, even if it takes *all the days of our lives.*

"Surely goodness and mercy shall follow me all the days of my life; and I will dwell in the house of the LORD forever" (Ps. 23:6 NKJV).

This must be one of the sweetest phrases ever penned. Can we read it from a few other translations?

"Goodness and love unfailing, these will follow me all the days of my life, and I shall dwell in the house of the LORD my whole life long" (NEB).

"I know that your goodness and love will be with me all my life; and your house will be my home as long as I live" (TEV).

"Your beauty and love chase after me every day of my life. I'm back home in the house of YAHWEH for the rest of my life" (MSG).

To read the verse is to open a box of jewels. Each word sparkles and begs to be examined in the face of our doubts: *goodness, mercy, all the days, dwell in the house of the LORD, forever.* They sweep in on insecurities like a SWAT team on a terrorist.

Look at the first word: *surely.* David didn't say, "*Maybe* goodness and mercy shall follow me." Or "*Possibly* goodness and mercy shall follow me." Or "*I have a hunch* that goodness and mercy shall follow me." David could have used one of those phrases. But he didn't. He believed in a sure God, who makes sure promises and provides a sure foundation. David would have loved the words of one of his great-great-grandsons, the apostle James. He described God as the one "with whom there is never the slightest variation or shadow of inconsistency" (James 1:17 PHILLIPS).

Our moods may shift, but God's doesn't. Our minds may change, but God's doesn't. Our devotion may falter, but God's never does. Even if we are faithless, he is faithful, for he cannot betray himself (2 Tim. 2:13). He is a sure God. And because he is a sure God, we can state confidently, "Surely goodness and mercy shall follow me all the days of my life."

And what follows the word *surely?* "Goodness and mercy." If the Lord is the shepherd who leads the flock, goodness and mercy are the two sheepdogs that guard the rear of the flock. Goodness *and* mercy. Not goodness alone, for we are sinners in need of mercy. Not mercy alone, for we are fragile, in need of goodness. We need them both. As one man wrote, "Goodness to supply every want. Mercy to forgive every sin. Goodness to provide. Mercy to pardon."[1]

Goodness and mercy—the celestial escort of God's flock. If that duo doesn't reinforce your faith, try this phrase: "all the days of my life."

What a huge statement. Look at the size of it! Goodness and mercy follow the child of God each and every day! Think of the days that lie ahead. What do you see? Days at home with only toddlers? God will be at your side. Days in a dead-end job? He will walk you through. Days of loneliness? He will take your hand. Surely goodness and mercy shall follow me—not some, not most, not nearly all—but all the days of my life.

And what will he do during those days? (Here is my favorite word.) He will "follow" you.

What a surprising way to describe God! We're accustomed to a God who remains in one place. A God who sits enthroned in the heavens and rules and ordains. David, however, envisions a mobile and active God. Dare we do the same? Dare we envision a God who follows us? Who pursues us? Who chases us? Who tracks us down and wins us over? Who follows us with "goodness and mercy" all the days of our lives?

Isn't this the kind of God described in the Bible? A God who follows us? There are many in the Scriptures who would say so. You have to go no farther than the third chapter of the first book before you find God in the role of a seeker. Adam and Eve are hiding in the bushes, partly to cover their bodies, partly to cover their sin. But does God wait for them to come to him? No, the words ring in the garden: "Where are you?" (Gen. 3:9). With that question God began a quest for the heart of humanity that continues up to and through the moment you read these words.

Moses can tell you about it. He was forty years in the desert when he looked over his shoulder and saw a bush blazing. God had followed him into the wilderness.

Jonah can tell you about it. He was a fugitive on a boat when he looked over his shoulder and saw clouds brewing. God had followed him onto the ocean.

The disciples of Jesus knew the feeling of being followed by God. They were rain soaked and shivering when they looked over their shoulders and saw Jesus walking toward them. God had followed them into the storm.

An unnamed Samaritan woman knew the same. She was alone in life and alone at the well when she looked over her shoulder and heard a Messiah speaking. God had followed her through her pain.

John the Apostle was banished on Patmos when he looked over his shoulder and saw the skies begin to open. God had followed him into his exile.

Lazarus was three days dead in a sealed tomb when he heard a voice, lifted his head, and looked over his shoulder and saw Jesus standing. God had followed him into death.

Peter had denied his Lord and gone back to fishing when he heard his name and looked over his shoulder and saw Jesus cooking breakfast. God had followed him in spite of his failure.

God is the God who follows. I wonder . . . have you sensed him following you? We often miss him. Like Eric, we don't know our Helper when he is near. But he comes.

Through the kindness of a stranger. The majesty of a sunset. The mystery of romance. Through the question of a child or the commitment of a spouse. Through a word well spoken or a touch well timed, have you sensed his presence?

If so, then release your doubts. Set them down. Be encumbered by them no longer. You are no candidate for insecurity. You are no longer a client of timidity. You can trust God. He has given his love to you; why don't you give your doubts to him?

Not easy to trust, you say? Maybe not, but neither is it as difficult as you think. Try these ideas:

Trust your faith and not your feelings. You don't feel spiritual each day? Of course you don't. But your feelings have no impact on God's presence. On the days you don't feel close to God, trust your faith and not your feelings. Goodness and mercy shall follow you all the days of your life.

Measure your value through God's eyes, not your own. To everyone else, Eric Hill was a homeless drifter. But to Debbie, he was a brother. There are times in our lives when we are gangrels—homeless, disoriented, hard to help, and hard to love. In those seasons remember this simple fact: God loves you. He follows you. Why? Because you are family, and he will follow you all the days of your life.

See the big picture, not the small. Eric's home was taken. His health was taken. But through the tragedy, his family was returned to him. Perhaps your home and health have been threatened as well. The immediate result might be pain. But the long-term result might be finding a Father you never knew. A Father who will follow you all the days of your life.

By the way, the last chapter in Eric Hill's life is the best one. Days before he died he recognized Debbie as his sister. And, in doing so, he discovered his home.

We will as well. Like Eric, we have doubted our Helper. But like Debbie, God has followed us. Like Eric, we are quick to turn away. But like Debbie, God is slow to anger and determined to stay. Like Eric, we don't accept God's gifts. But like Debbie, God still gives them. He gives us his angels, not just pinned on a lapel, but placed on our path.

And most of all, God gives us himself. Even when we choose our hovel over his house and our trash over his grace, still he follows. Never forcing us. Never leaving us. Patiently persistent. Faithfully present. Using all of his power to convince us that he is who he is and that he can be trusted to lead us home.

His goodness and mercy will follow us all the days of our lives.

18

Almost Heaven

The Burden of Homesickness

I will dwell in the house of the LORD forever.

PSALM 23:6 NKJV

F or the last twenty years, I've wanted a dog. A big dog. But there were always problems. The apartment was too small. The budget was too tight. The girls were too young. But most of all, Denalyn was unenthusiastic. Her logic? She'd already married one slobbering, shedding beast, why put up with a second? So we compromised and got a small dog.

I like Salty, but small dogs aren't really dogs. They don't bark; they yelp. They don't eat; they nibble. They don't lick you; they sniff you. I like Salty, but I wanted a real dog. A man's-best-friend type of dog. A fat-pawed, big-eating, slurp-you-on-the-face type of dog you could saddle or wrestle or both.

I was alone in my passion until Sara was born. She loves dogs. And the two of us were able to sway the household vote. Denalyn gave in, and Sara and I began the search. We discovered a woman in South Carolina who breeds golden retrievers in a Christian environment. From birth the dogs are surrounded by inspirational music and prayers. (No, I don't know if they tithe with dog biscuits.) When the trainer told me that she had read my books, I got on board. A woman with such good taste is bound to be a good breeder, right?

So we ordered a pup. We mailed the check, selected the name Molly, and cleared a corner for her dog pillow. The dog hadn't even been born, and she was named, claimed, and given a place in the house.

Can't the same be said about you? Long before your first whimper, your Master claimed you, named you, and hung a reserved sign on your room. You and Molly have more in common than odor and eating habits. (Just teasing.)

You're both being groomed for a trip. We prefer the terms *maturation* and *sanctification* to *weaning* and *training,* but it's all the same. You're being prepared for your Master's house. You don't know the departure date or flight number, but you can bet your puppy chow that you'll be seeing your Owner someday. Isn't this the concluding promise of David?

"And I will dwell in the house of the LORD forever" (Ps. 23:6 NKJV).

Where will you live forever? In the house of the Lord. If his house is your "forever house," what does that make this earthly house? You got it! Short-term housing. This is not our home. "Our homeland is in heaven" (Phil. 3:20).

This explains the homesickness we feel.

Have you ever longed to be home? May I share a time when I did? I was spending the summer of my nineteenth year working in northern Georgia. The folks in that region are very nice, but no one is too nice to a door-to-door salesman. There were times that summer when I was so lonely for home I felt my bones would melt.

One of those occasions came on the side of a country road. The hour was late, and I was lost. I'd stopped to pull out a flashlight and a map. To my right was a farmhouse. In the farmhouse was a family. I knew it was a family because I could see them. Right through the big plate-glass window, I could see the mother and father and boy and girl. Norman Rockwell would have placed them on a canvas. The mom was spooning out food, and the dad was telling a story, and the kids were laughing, and it was all I could do to keep from ringing the doorbell and asking for a place at the table. I felt so far from home.

What I felt that night, some of you have felt ever since . . .

your husband died.

your child was buried.

you learned about the lump in your breast or the spot in your lung.

Some of you have felt far from home ever since your home fell apart.

The twists and turns of life have a way of reminding us—we aren't home here. This is not our homeland. We aren't fluent in the languages of disease and death. The culture confuses the heart, the noise disrupts our sleep, and we feel far from home.

And, you know what? That's OK.

Homesickness is one of the burdens God doesn't mind if we carry. We, like Molly, are being prepared for another house. And we, like the parakeet from Green Bay, know we aren't there yet.

Pootsie was her name. She escaped from her owner and came into the keeping of the humane society. When no one else claimed her, Sue Gleason did. They hit it off. They talked and bathed together, becoming fast friends. But one day the little bird did something incredible. It flew over to Mrs. Gleason, put her beak in her ear, and whispered, "Fifteen hundred South Oneida Street, Green Bay."

Gleason was dumbfounded. She researched and found that the address existed. She went to the house and found a seventy-nine-year-old man named John Stroobants.

"Do you have a parakeet?" she asked.

"I used to; I miss him terribly."

When he saw his Pootsie, he was thrilled. "You know, he even knows his phone number."[1]

The story isn't as crazy as you might think. You have an eternal address fixed in your mind as well. God has "set eternity in the hearts of men" (Eccles. 3:11 NIV). Down deep you know you are not home yet.

So be careful not to act like you are. Don't lower the duffel bag too soon. Would you hang pictures on the wall of a Greyhound bus? Do you set up a bedroom at the roadside rest stop? Do you load your king-size bed on a commercial flight?

Would you treat this world like home? It isn't. The greatest calamity is not to feel far from home when you are, but to feel right at home when you are not. Don't quench, but rather, stir this longing for heaven.

God's home is a *forever* home. "And I will dwell in the house of the LORD forever" (Ps. 23:6 NKJV).

My friends Jeff and Carol just adopted two small children. Christopher, the older, is only three, but he knows the difference between Jeff's house and the foster home from which he came. He tells all visitors, "This is my forever home."

Won't it be great when we say the same? Couldn't we use a forever home? This home we're in won't last forever. Birthdays remind us of that.

During the writing of this book I turned forty-six. I'm closer to ninety than I am to infancy. All those things they say about aging are coming true. I'm patting myself less on the back and more under the chin. I have everything I had twenty years ago, except now it's all lower. The other day I tried to straighten out the wrinkles in my socks and found out I wasn't wearing any. I can relate to Dave Barry's description of aging:

> . . . dental problems, intestinal malfunctions, muscle deterioration, emotional instability, memory lapses, hearing and vision loss, impotence, seizures, growths, prostate problems, greatly reduced limb function, massive coronary failure, death, and, of course, painful hemorrhoidal swelling.[2]

Aging. It's no fun. The way we try to avoid it, you'd think we could. We paint the body, preserve the body, protect the body. And well we should. These bodies are God's gifts. We should be responsible. But we should also be realistic. This body must die so the new body can live. "Flesh and blood cannot have a part in the kingdom of God. Something that will ruin cannot have a part in something that never ruins" (1 Cor. 15:50).

Aging is God's idea. It's one of the ways he keeps us headed homeward. We can't change the process, but we can change our attitude. Here is a thought. What if we looked at the aging body as we look at the growth of a tulip?

Do you ever see anyone mourning over the passing of the tulip bulb? Do gardeners weep as the bulb begins to weaken? Of course not. We don't purchase tulip girdles or petal wrinkle cream or consult plastic-leaf surgeons. We don't mourn the passing of the bulb; we celebrate it. Tulip lovers rejoice the minute the bulb weakens. "Watch that one," they say. "It's about to blossom."

Could it be heaven does the same? The angels point to our bodies. The more frail we become, the more excited they become. "Watch that lady in the hospital," they say. "She's about to blossom." "Keep an eye on the fellow with the bad heart. He'll be coming home soon."

"We are waiting for God to finish making us his own children, which means our bodies will be made free" (Rom. 8:23).

Are our bodies now free? No. Paul describes them as our "earthy bodies" (Phil. 3:21 MSG). Or as other translations state:

"our lowly body" (NKJV)

"the body of our humble state" (NASB)

"these weak mortal bodies" (NLT)

"our vile body" (KJV)

"our simple bodies" (NCV)

You could add your own adjective, couldn't you? Which word describes your body? My *cancerous* body? My *arthritic* body? My *deformed* body? My *crippled* body? My *addicted* body? My *ever-expanding* body? The word may be different, but the message is the same: These bodies are weak. They began decaying the minute we began breathing.

And, according to God, that's a part of the plan. Every wrinkle and every needle take us one step closer to the last step when Jesus will change our simple bodies into forever bodies. No pain. No depression. No sickness. No end.

This is not our forever house. It will serve for the time being. But there is nothing like the moment we enter his door.

Molly can tell you. After a month in our house she ran away. I came home one night to find the place unusually quiet. Molly was gone.

She'd slipped out unnoticed. The search began immediately. Within an hour we knew that she was far, far from home. Now, if you don't like pets, what I'm about to say is going to sound strange. If you do like pets, you will understand.

You'll understand why we walked up and down the street, calling her name. You'll understand why I drove around the neighborhood at 10:30 P.M. You'll understand why I put up a poster in the convenience store and convened the family for a prayer. (Honestly, I did.) You'll understand why I sent e-mails to the staff, asking for prayers, and to her breeder, asking for advice. And you'll understand why we were ready to toss the confetti and party when she showed up.

Here is what happened. The next morning Denalyn was on her way home from taking the girls to school when she saw the trash truck. She asked the workers to keep an eye out for Molly and then hurried home to host a moms' prayer group. Soon after the ladies arrived, the trash truck pulled into our driveway, a worker opened the door, and out bounded our dog. She had been found.

When Denalyn called to tell me the news, I could barely hear her voice. It was Mardi Gras in the kitchen. The ladies were celebrating the return of Molly.

This story pops with symbolism. The master leaving his house, searching for the lost. Victories in the midst of prayer. Great things coming out of trash. But most of all: the celebration at the coming home. That's something else you have in common with Molly—a party at your homecoming.

By that moment only one bag will remain. Not guilt. It was dropped at Calvary. Not the fear of death. It was left at the grave. The only lingering luggage will be this God-given longing for home. And when you see him, you'll set it down. Just as a returning soldier drops his duffel when he sees his wife, you'll drop your longing when you see your Father. Those you love will shout. Those you know will applaud. But all the noise will cease when he cups your chin and says, "Welcome home." And with scarred hand he'll wipe every tear from your eye. And you will dwell in the house of your Lord—forever.

Conclusion

I fell asleep in the Louvre.

The most famous museum in the world. The best-known building in Paris. Tourists are oohing and aahing, and that's me, nodding and snoring. Seated on a bench. Back to the wall. Chin to my chest. Conked out.

The crown jewels are down the hall. Rembrandt is on the wall. Van Gogh is one floor up. The *Venus de Milo* is one floor down. I should have been star struck and wide eyed.

Denalyn was. You'd have thought she was at Foley's Red Apple sale. If there was a tour, she took it. If there was a button to push, she pushed it. If there was a brochure to read, she read it. She didn't even want to stop to eat.

But me? I gave the *Mona Lisa* five minutes. ·

Shameful, I know.

I should have been more like the fellow next to me. When I dozed off, he was transfixed on a seventeenth-century Dutch artist's rendering of a flower. When I awoke, the guy was still staring. I closed my eyes again. When I opened them, he hadn't moved.

I leaned toward him and tried to sound reflective. "Awesome, eh?" No response. "The shades are masterful." Still no reply. "Do you think it's a number painting?" He sighed and said nothing, but I knew what he was thinking, *Uncultured klutz.*

He's right. I was. But it wasn't my fault. I like seventeenth-century art as much as the next guy . . . well, maybe not that much. But at least I can usually stay awake.

But not that day. Why did I fall asleep at the Louvre?

Blame it on the bags, baby; blame it on the bags. I was worn out from lugging the family luggage. We checked more suitcases than the road show of the *Phantom of the Opera*.

I can't fault my wife and daughters. They learned it from me. Remember, I'm the one who travels prepared for an underwater wedding and a bowling tournament. It's bad enough for one person to travel like that, but five? It'll wear you out.

You think I'll ever learn to travel light?

I tell you what. Let's make a pact. I'll reduce the leather bags, and we'll both reduce the emotional ones. After all, it's one thing to sleep through the Louvre but quite another to sleep through life.

We can, you know. Do we not dwell in the gallery of our God? Isn't the sky his canvas and humanity his magnum opus? Are we not encircled by artistry? Sunsets burning. Waves billowing.

And isn't the soul his studio? The birthing of love, the bequeathing of grace. All around us miracles pop like fireflies—souls are touched, hearts are changed, and . . .

Yawn. We miss it. We sleep through it. We can't help it. It's hard work carrying yesterday's guilt around. This burlap bag of worry has my neck in a knot. The dread of death is enough to break a back.

It's also enough to make you miss the magic of life. Many miss it every Sunday. Good, well-meaning folks sitting in church, fighting to keep the eyes—if not of their heads at least of their hearts—awake.

And what do we miss? We miss God parting the heavens to hear us sing. Shouldn't we be stretching heavenward, tiptoed on our pews?

What do we miss? God is meeting us in communion! Shouldn't we be distributing, along with the wafers and wine, ammonia sticks so we could awaken each other from our faints of awe?

What do we miss? God's Word. Should we not hold it like nitroglycerin? Shouldn't we be wide-awake? We should, but we dragged that trunk of dissatisfaction all over town last week. And, besides that, we couldn't sleep last night; we kept rolling over on our duffel bag of disappointments.

Then let's get rid of the bags! Once and for all, let's give our luggage to him. Let's take him at his word! "Come to me, all of you who are weary and carry heavy burdens, and I will give you rest" (Matt. 11:28 NLT).

Rest from the burden of a small god. Why? Because I have found **the Lord.**

Rest from doing things my way. Why? Because **the Lord is my Shepherd.**

Rest from endless wants. Why? Because **I shall not want.**

Rest from weariness. Why? Because **he makes me to lie down.**

Rest from worry. Why? Because **he leads me.**

Rest from hopelessness. Why? Because **he restores my soul.**

Rest from guilt. Why? Because **he leads me in the paths of righteousness.**

Rest from arrogance. Why? Because of **his name's sake.**

Rest from the valley of death. Why? Because **he walks me through it.**

Rest from the shadow of grief. Why? Because **he guides me.**

Rest from fear. Why? Because **his presence comforts me.**

Rest from loneliness. Why? Because **he is with me.**

Rest from shame. Why? Because **he has prepared a place for me in the presence of my enemies.**

Rest from my disappointments. Why? Because **he anoints me.**

Rest from envy. Why? Because **my cup overflows.**

Rest from doubt. Why? Because **he follows me.**

Rest from homesickness. Why? Because **I will dwell in the house of my Lord forever.**

And tomorrow, when out of habit you pick your luggage back up, set it down again. Set it down again and again until that sweet day when you find you aren't picking it back up.

And on that day, when you feel the load lifted, when you've taken a step toward traveling light, when you have the energy to ponder the mysteries of life, do me a favor. Walk down the hall and turn to the left. Wait your turn behind the scarlet ropes. Take a good, long look at the *Mona Lisa,* and tell me, what's the big deal about her anyway?

Notes

CHAPTER 2: THE MIDDLE C OF LIFE

1. Or, in Hebrew, fifty-four words describe the first one.

2. Around A.D. 200 Christian scholars began writing the vowels for *Adonai* beneath the Tetragrammaton (YHWH), reminding the reader to say "Adonai." The word was still unpronounceable until German scholars in the middle of the nineteenth century inserted the vowels of *Adonai* between the *Yahweh* consonants creating the name *Jehovah*—a name that had never existed in any language.

3. Nathan Stone, *Names of God* (Chicago: Moody Press, 1944), 20.

4. Donald W. McCullough, *The Trivialization of God: The Dangerous Illusion of a Manageable Deity* (Colorado Springs: NavPress, 1995), 66.

5. Ibid., 54.

CHAPTER 3: I'LL DO IT MY WAY

1. With appreciation to Rick Reilly and his chapter on Jean Van de Velde, *"Mon Dieu!* Better Safe Than Sorry!" in *The Life of Reilly* (New York: Total Sports Illustrated, 2000), 175–77.

CHAPTER 4: THE PRISON OF WANT

1. Randy C. Alcorn, *Money, Possessions, and Eternity* (Wheaton, Ill.: Tyndale Publishers, 1989), 55.

2. Chris Seidman, *Little Buddy* (Orange, Calif.: New Leaf Books, 2001), 138. Used with permission.

3. Rick Atchley, "I Have Learned the Secret," audiotape 7 of the 1997 Pepperdine Lectures (Malibu, Calif., 1997). Used with permission.

4. Used with permission.

Chapter 5: I Will Give You Rest

1. Robert Sullivan, "Sleepless in America," *Life*, February 1998, 56–66 and *Prime Time Live*, 2 March 1998.

2. Sullivan, "Sleepless," 63.

3. Ibid.

4. Phillip Keller, *A Shepherd Looks at Psalm 23* (Grand Rapids, Mich.: Zondervan Publishing, 1970; reprint, in *Phillip Keller: The Inspirational Writings*, New York: Inspirational Press, 1993), 28–29 (page citations are to the reprint edition).

5. Helmut Thielicke, *Encounter with Spurgeon*, trans. John W. Doberstein (Philadelphia: Fortress Press, 1963; reprint, Grand Rapids, Mich.: Baker Book House, 1975), 220 (page citation is to the reprint edition).

Chapter 6: Whaddifs and Howells

1. Og Mandino, *The Spellbinder's Gift* (New York: Fawcett Columbine, 1995), 70–71.

2. From "Worrier and Warrior," a sermon by Ted Schroder, Christ Episcopal Church, San Antonio, Texas, on 10 April 1994.

3. See Psalm 119:105.

Chapter 9: Get Over Yourself

1. Rick Reilly, *The Life of Reilly* (New York: Total Sports Illustrated, 2000), 73.

2. Paul Lee Tan, *Encyclopedia of 7700 Illustrations* (Rockville, Md.: Assurance Publishers, 1979), 211.

3. Ibid., 1100.

4. William J. Bennett, ed., *The Spirit of America: Words of Advice from the Founders in Stories, Letters, Poem and Speeches* (New York: Touchstone, 1997), 161.

CHAPTER 10: I WILL LEAD YOU HOME

1. Phillip Keller, *A Shepherd Looks at Psalm 23* (Grand Rapids, Mich.: Zondervan Publishing, 1970; reprint, in *Phillip Keller: The Inspirational Writings*, New York: Inspirational Press, 1993), 70 (page citation is to the reprint edition).

2. F. W. Boreham, *Life Verses: The Bible's Impact on Famous Lives,* vol. 2 (Grand Rapids, Mich.: Kregel Publications, 1994), 211.

CHAPTER 11: WHEN MOURNING COMES

1. Michael P. Green, ed., *Illustrations for Biblical Preaching* (Grand Rapids, Mich.: Baker Book House, 1989), 91.

CHAPTER 14: THE CROWING ROOSTER AND ME

1. Charles W. Slemming, *He Leadeth Me: The Shepherd's Life in Palestine* (Fort Washington, Pa.: Christian Literature Crusade, 1964), quoted in Charles R. Swindoll, *Living Beyond the Daily Grind, Book 1: Reflections on the Songs and Sayings in Scripture* (Nashville: W Publishing Group, 1988), 77–78.

CHAPTER 15: SLIPPERY SHEEP AND HEALED HURTS

1. "Paul was in prison several times: Philippi (Acts 16:23); Jerusalem (Acts 23:18); Caesarea (Acts 23:33; 24:27; 25:14); and Rome (Acts 28:16, 20, 30)." Robert B. Hughes and J. Carl Laney, *New Bible Companion* (Wheaton, Ill.: Tyndale House Publishers, 1990), 681.

2. Phillip Keller, *A Shepherd Looks at Psalm 23* (Grand Rapids, Mich.: Zondervan Publishing, 1970; reprint, in *Phillip Keller: The Inspirational Writings,* New York: Inspirational Press, 1993), 99 (page citation is to the reprint edition).

CHAPTER 16: JAM SESSION

1. F. B. Meyer, *The Shepherd Psalm* (Grand Rapids, Mich.: Kregel Publications, 1991), 115.

2. From a sermon entitled "God's Antidote to Your Hurt" by Rick Warren.

CHAPTER 17: GOD'S LOVING PURSUIT

1. F. B. Meyer, *The Shepherd Psalm* (Grand Rapids, Mich.: Kregel Publications, 1991), 125.

2. Though originally written for this book, this story initially appeared in *The Gift for All People.* Thanks to Multnomah Publishing for allowing us to use it in *Traveling Light.*

CHAPTER 18: ALMOST HEAVEN

1. Calvin Miller, *Into the Depths of God: Where Eyes See the Invisible, Ears Hear the Inaudible, and Minds Conceive the Inconceivable* (Minneapolis: Bethany House, 2000), 217.

2. Dave Barry, *Dave Barry Turns 40* (New York: Crown, 1990), quoted in Helen Exley, *A Spread of Over 40s Jokes* (New York: Exley Giftbooks, 1992).

Study Guide

Traveling Light

Prepared by Steve Halliday

1

The Luggage of Life

TRAVELING BACK

1. *The bags we grab are not made of leather; they're made of burdens. The suitcase of guilt. A sack of discontent. You drape a duffel bag of weariness on one shoulder and a hanging bag of grief on the other. Add on a backpack of doubt, an overnight bag of loneliness, and a trunk of fear. Pretty soon you're pulling more stuff than a skycap. No wonder you're so tired at the end of the day. Lugging luggage is exhausting.*

   A. Which of the "bags" listed here trouble you the most? Why?

   B. Have you left any luggage behind? How did it feel to do so?

2. *God is saying to you, "Set that stuff down! You're carrying burdens you don't need to bear."*

   A. Why do you think we carry burdens we don't need to bear?

   B. What keeps you from setting down burdens you needn't bear?

3. *Traveling light means trusting God with the burdens you were never intended to bear.*

   A. What does it mean to trust God with a burden? How does one do this?

   B. What have you learned from observing others with their "luggage"?

TRAVELING UP

1. Read Psalm 23.

   A. What pictures leap to mind when you read this psalm?

   B. What memories does this psalm conjure up for you?

   C. What part of this psalm means the most to you? Why?

   D. How does this psalm teach us to give up personal burdens?

2. Read Matthew 11:28–30.

   A. To whom are these words addressed? Does this include you?

   B. What promise does Jesus give to those who respond to his invitation?

   C. Are you taking advantage of Jesus' invitation? Why or why not?

3. Read 1 Peter 5:7.

   A. What does this verse instruct us to do? (How are we to obey?)

   B. What reason does Peter give for obeying this command?

   C. What benefit can we expect to receive when we obey?

TRAVELING ON

1. Set aside at least a half-hour for prayer, and ask the Lord to reveal any burdens you need to lay down. Pray with a piece of paper and a pen in hand, and write down any burdens the Lord brings to mind. Show your completed list to your closest friend, and ask him or her to pray with you that God will show you how to release these burdens.

2. What burdens are your loved ones needlessly bearing? What can you do to help them lay down those unnecessary burdens?

2

The Middle C of Life

The Burden of a Lesser God

TRAVELING BACK

1. *With his very first words in [Psalm 23], David sets out to deliver us from the burden of a lesser deity.*

   A. What lesser deities hold an attraction for your acquaintances?

   B. Why would anyone settle for a lesser deity?

2. Max says that many people settle for one of three lesser deities: God as a genie in a bottle, as a sweet grandpa, or as a busy dad.

   A. Describe in your own words each of these lesser deities. What seems attractive about them?

   B. Have any of these three lesser deities appealed to you? Why or why not?

3. *God is the "One who is" and the "One who causes." Why is that important? Because we need a big God. And if God is the "One who is," then he is an unchanging God.*

   A. Why do we need a big God? Why do we need an unchanging God?

   B. What would be different about your life if God were smaller than he is? How would you feel if he changed capriciously?

4. *Unchanging. Uncaused. Ungoverned. These are only a fraction of God's qualities, but aren't they enough to give you a glimpse of your Father? Don't we need this kind of shepherd? Don't we need an unchanging shepherd?*

   A. How do you answer Max's questions?

   B. Give an example of how God has been an unchanging shepherd in your life.

Traveling Up

1. Read Exodus 3:13–17; 6:2–8.

   A. What do you learn about God from his name?

   B. What do you learn about God from his track record?

   C. What do you learn about God's concern for his people?

2. Read Psalm 102:25–27; 139:7–12.

   A. What do you learn about God from these passages? How do these verses affect your view of God?

3. Read 1 Timothy 6:13–16.

   A. What do you learn about God from this text?

   B. How does Paul suggest we respond to this God?

4. Read Isaiah 40:21–31.

   A. What does this text reveal about God?

   B. What does God think of pretenders to his throne?

   C. How does God intend for this majestic picture of him to encourage our weary hearts?

Traveling On

1. Do a study on the false gods described in Scripture. Start with names such as "Chemosh," "Baal," "Asherah," and the generic "gods." Do other research, perhaps in a good Bible dictionary, to discover something about these "lesser gods." How do they compare to the God of Jesus?

2. Spend some time meditating and concentrating on the attributes of the real God of the Bible. Consider using a daily devotional such as *How Great Thou Art* (Sister, Ore.: Multnomah, 1999), which focuses for a full year on the majesty and greatness of God.

3

—

I'll Do It My Way

The Burden of Self-Reliance

TRAVELING BACK

1. *We humans want to do things our way. Forget the easy way. Forget the common way. Forget the best way. Forget God's way. We want to do things our way.*

   A. What is it about us that causes us to desire our own way?

   B. When we rely on ourselves rather than God, what is the result?

2. *When David, who was a warrior, minstrel, and ambassador for God, searched for an illustration of God, he remembered his days as a shepherd. . . . And the way he cared for the sheep reminded him of the way God cares for us. David rejoiced to say, "The LORD is my shepherd," and in so doing he proudly implied, "I am his sheep."*

   A. Why do you think David chose to picture God through the image of a shepherd? Why not use another image?

   B. Do you proudly think of yourself as a sheep? Explain.

3. *Will you humor me and take a simple quiz? See if you succeed in self-reliance. Raise your hand if any of the following describe you.*

   You can control your moods.
   You are at peace with everyone.
   You have no fears.
   You need no forgiveness.

   A. Describe someone you know who believes he or she fits one of the previous four statements.

B. Which of these four areas of life cause you the most struggles? Explain.

C. Why is it that the ones who most need a shepherd resist him so?

TRAVELING UP

1. Read Jeremiah 17:5–8.

    A. What does the Lord think of someone who relies on himself (v. 5)?

    B. What is the result of relying on yourself (v. 6)?

    C. How does the Lord feel about those who trust in him (v. 7)?

    D. What is the result of trusting in God (v. 8)?

2. Read Deuteronomy 8:10–18.

    A. What are we to do in times of prosperity (v. 10)?

    B. In what way can prosperity create a spiritual threat (vv. 11–14)?

    C. Why is it always foolish to believe that we are self-sufficient (vv. 15–18)?

3. Read 1 Corinthians 4:6–7.

    A. What does it mean to "not go beyond what is written" (v. 6 NIV)? Why does the Bible warn us to "not go beyond what is written"?

    B. How would you answer Paul's three questions in verse 7?

TRAVELING ON

1. Consciously get out of your comfort zone, and do something that requires you to rely on another person. Make it as exotic as a parachute jump or as mundane as asking directions to a place you've never visited.

2. Read the classic *A Shepherd Looks at Psalm 23* by Phillip Keller to gain a better picture of what it means to be a sheep in the fold of God.

4

The Prison of Want

The Burden of Discontent

TRAVELING BACK

1. *The prison of want. You've seen her prisoners. They are "in want." They want something. They want something bigger. Nicer. Faster. Thinner. They want.*

   A. Are you in prison?

   B. What things in life are most likely to send you to this prison? Describe them.

2. *David has found the pasture where discontent goes to die. It's as if he is saying, "What I have in God is greater than what I don't have in life."*

   A. What do you have in God? List the first ten things that come to mind.

   B. Can you say that what you have in God is greater than what you don't have in life? Explain.

3. *Are you hoping that a change in circumstances will bring a change in your attitude? If so, you are in prison, and you need to learn a secret of traveling light.*

   A. Answer the question above and explain your answer.

   B. What is this secret of traveling light? How does one master it?

4. *What is the one thing separating you from joy? How do you fill in this blank: "I will be happy when _____"? When I am healed. When I am promoted. When I am married. When I am single. When I am rich. How would you finish that statement?*

   A. Answer the question above.

B. How does this thing separate you from joy? How long has it been doing so? How can you deprive it of its power over you?

Traveling Up

1. Read Luke 12:13–21.

   A. What warning does Jesus give in verse 15? What declaration does he make?

   B. What error did the rich man make in the parable Jesus told?

   C. What does it mean to be "rich toward God" (v. 21)? Are you rich toward God? Explain.

2. Read Philippians 4:10–13.

   A. Why did Paul "rejoice greatly in the Lord" (v. 10 NIV)?

   B. What secret does Paul describe in verse 12? How did he gain access to this secret? Do you know this secret? Explain.

   C. How does verse 13 relate to the context of the passage? How does it relate specifically to contentment?

3. Read 1 Timothy 6:3–10.

   A. How does Paul characterize those who teach that godliness is a means to financial gain (v. 5)?

   B. What does Paul say is "great gain" (v. 6 NIV)?

   C. What reason does Paul give for his statement (vv. 7–8)?

   D. What warning does Paul give in verses 9–10? Why do so many people ignore this warning? What do you think of his warning? Explain.

Traveling On

1. Make a list of at least a dozen things you possess, whether spiritual or material, that came to you as a result of your relationship with God.

2. Do a Bible study on contentment. Use a good concordance to look up words such as *content* and *contented*, then study the verses that you find. Also see what a good Bible dictionary or encyclopedia has to say on the topic. What do you learn?

5

I Will Give You Rest

The Burden of Weariness

TRAVELING BACK

1. *People with too much work and too little sleep step over to the baggage claim of life and grab the duffel bag of weariness. You don't carry this one. You don't hoist it onto your shoulder and stride down the street. You drag it as you would a stubborn St. Bernard.*

    A. What sorts of things tend to make you weary?

    B. How do you normally deal with weariness? What did you do the last time weariness struck hard?

2. *In our book, busyness is next to godliness. We idolize Thomas Edison, who claimed he could live on fifteen-minute naps. Somehow we forget to mention Albert Einstein, who averaged eleven hours of sleep a night.*

    A. How often do you tell others, "I'm really busy right now"? What keeps you so busy?

    B. How much sleep do you normally get? Is it sufficient for you to function well? Explain.

3. *God's message is plain: "If creation didn't crash when I rested, it won't crash when you do." Repeat these words after me: It is not my job to run the world.*

    A. Name some of the reasons you have heard (or used yourself) for not getting adequate rest.

    B. Why do you think God so emphasized the fourth commandment, about resting on the Sabbath day?

4. *In a world rocky with human failure, there is a land lush with divine mercy. Your Shepherd invites you there. He wants you to lie down. Nestle*

*deeply until you are hidden, buried, in the tall shoots of his love, and
there you will find rest.*

A. What is your favorite way of nestling deeply "in the tall shoots
   of his love"? Describe what most refreshes you.

B. What is keeping you from resting in God's love right now?

Traveling Up

1. Read Exodus 20:8–11.

   A. What does it mean to keep the Sabbath day "holy"?

   B. What does God command Israel in verses 9–10?

   C. What reason does God give in verse 11 for his command?

   D. Why do you think God so highly values our rest?

2. Read Isaiah 30:15–18.

   A. According to verse 15, Israel's salvation consisted in what?
      How did the nation respond to this direction?

   B. What response is described in verse 16? How do we often
      respond in a similar way?

   C. What is the result of ignoring God's command to rest (v. 17)?

   D. Despite our foolishness, how does the Lord treat us (v. 18)?

3. Read Hebrews 4:1–11.

   A. What does the writer warn us about in verse 1?

   B. What keeps people from entering God's rest (vv. 2–6)?

   C. When is the best time to obey God's command (v. 7)?

   D. What kind of rest is the writer describing in verse 9?

   E. How do we "labour" to enter God's rest (v. 11 KJV)?

Traveling On

1. What activities or events keep you busy? Try an experiment to
   judge the accuracy of your assumptions. Keep a "busyness journal"

for one week, recording the things that occupy your time. Write down not only what you did but also how long each took. Then at the end of the week evaluate your journal. Are you busy doing the things that matter most? Or do you need to make some changes?

2. How much sleep do you get? Keep a chart for one month, accurately recording the amount and quality of your sleep. Do the results surprise you? What changes, if any, do you need to make?

6

Whaddifs and Howells

The Burden of Worry

TRAVELING BACK

1. *Worry is the burlap bag of burdens. It's overflowing with "whaddifs" and "howells." "Whaddif it rains at my wedding?" "Howell I know when to discipline my kids?" "Whaddif I marry a guy who snores?" "Howell we pay our baby's tuition?"*

    A. What "whaddifs" trouble you the most?

    B. What "howells" give you the most grief?

    C. How do you typically deal with these "whaddifs" and "howells"?

2. *Worry divides the mind. The biblical word for worry (merimnao) is a compound of two Greek words, merizo ("to divide") and nous ("the mind"). Anxiety splits our energy between today's priorities and tomorrow's problems. Part of our mind is on the now; the rest is on the not yet. The result is half-minded living.*

    A. What practical things can we do to keep from spending today's energies on tomorrow's problems?

    B. What issues are most likely to nudge you toward half-minded living? Why?

3. *God leads us. God will do the right thing at the right time. And what a difference that makes.*

    A. How has God led you in the past? Describe at least one incident.

    B. Do we believe that God will do the right thing at the right time? How would our lives change if we really believed this?

C. What in your life would change *right now* if you believed this fully?

4. *Meet today's problems with today's strength. Don't start tackling tomorrow's problems until tomorrow. You do not have tomorrow's strength yet. You simply have enough for today.*

   A. How many of the things you have worried about actually have come to pass?

   B. What issues that should be dealt with today are you avoiding by trying to tackle tomorrow's problems?

TRAVELING UP

1. Read Matthew 6:25–34.

   A. What reason does Jesus give for refusing to worry (vv. 25–27)?

   B. Why should worry not trouble Christians in the same way it troubles nonbelievers (vv. 31–32)?

   C. If we are not to worry, what are we to do (v. 33)? What does this mean in practical terms?

   D. What additional reason for not worrying does Jesus give in verse 34?

2. Read Philippians 4:6–8.

   A. How does Paul recommend that we combat worry?

   B. According to Paul, what will we enjoy when we follow his counsel?

   C. Rather than worry, what kinds of things should fill our minds (v. 8)?

3. Read Hebrews 4:14–16.

   A. Describe the high priest pictured in this passage.

   B. How is verse 16 designed to combat our worry?

TRAVELING ON

1. Make a list of the things in life that worry you the most. Then, one by one, commit these items to the Lord in prayer. As you pray for each concern, tear it off your sheet of paper and throw it in the trash.

2. Use a good concordance to do a word study on worry. Look up terms such as *worry*, *worried*, *anxious*, and *anxiety*, and study the verses that you find. What do you learn about how to combat worry?

7

It's a Jungle Out There

The Burden of Hopelessness

TRAVELING BACK

1. *Hopelessness is an odd bag. Unlike the others, it isn't full. It is empty, and its emptiness creates the burden. Unzip the top and examine all the pockets. Turn it upside down and shake it hard. The bag of hopelessness is painfully empty.*

   A. Describe a time when you felt hopeless. What made you feel that way?

   B. What in your life right now threatens your hope? How will you deal with it?

2. *If you have only a person but no renewed vision, all you have is company. If he has a vision but no direction, you have a dreamer for company. But if you have a person with direction—who can take you from this place to the right place—ah, then you have one who can restore your hope.*

   A. Why does it take a competent guide to restore hope?

   B. Do you have such a guide? Explain.

3. *God, your rescuer, has the right vision. He also has the right direction. He made the boldest claim in the history of man when he declared, "I am the way."*

   A. What did Jesus mean when he said, "I am the way"?

   B. Why wasn't it arrogant of Jesus to say that he was *the* way? Then what about Muhammad, the Dalai Lama, or spiritual leaders of other faiths?

4. *We ask God, "Where are you taking me? Where is the path?" And he, like the guide, doesn't tell us. Oh, he may give us a hint or two, but that's*

all. If he did, would we understand? Would we comprehend our location? No, like the traveler, we are unacquainted with this jungle. So rather than give us an answer, Jesus gives us a far greater gift. He gives us himself.

A. How does it make you feel that God almost never tells us what lies ahead for us? Do you wish he did things differently? Explain.

B. In what ways has Jesus guided you in the past? How are you depending upon his guidance right now?

TRAVELING UP

1. Read Psalm 121.

   A. From where did the psalmist expect his hope to arrive (v. 2)?

   B. How much sleep does God get each night (vv. 3–4)? Why is this important?

   C. What kinds of things is the Lord said to watch over in verses 5–8? How can this give you hope?

2. Read Psalm 33:16–22.

   A. What *cannot* save a king or a warrior (vv. 16–17)? Why are these things vain hopes?

   B. On whom does the Lord fix his eyes (v. 18)? What difference does this make?

   C. What does it mean to "wait in hope" (v. 20 NIV)? How can you put your hope in the Lord?

3. Read Romans 8:18–25.

   A. Why should we avoid attaching too much importance to our present sufferings (v. 18)?

   B. Why do we need hope in the first place (vv. 19–23)?

   C. How does Paul define real hope (v. 24)?

   D. Why is it always too soon to give up hope (v. 25)?

Traveling On

1. Take a guided tour of a place you've never visited. During the tour, consciously remind yourself of how your Savior desires to guide you through life. What unexpected discoveries or parallels do you uncover?

2. Do a Bible study on hope. Use a good concordance to look up the word *hope* and its derivatives, like *hoping, hoped, hopeful,* etc. What do you learn?

8

A Heavenly Exchange

The Burden of Guilt

TRAVELING BACK

1. *God is never wrong. He has never rendered a wrong decision, experienced the wrong attitude, taken the wrong path, said the wrong thing, or acted the wrong way. He is never too late or too early, too loud or too soft, too fast or too slow. He has always been and always will be right. He is righteous.*

   A. Has it ever felt as if God made a mistake with your life? If so, how did you deal with this feeling?

   B. Who is the most "righteous" person you know? What makes you say this about him or her?

2. *The weight of weariness pulls you down. Self-reliance misleads you. Disappointments discourage you. Anxiety plagues you. But guilt? Guilt consumes you. So what do we do? Our Lord is right, and we are wrong. His party is for the guiltless, and we are anything but. What do we do?*

   A. Answer the question above.

   B. How do you deal with disappointments? With anxiety? Guilt?

3. *It was, at once, history's most beautiful and most horrible moment. Jesus stood in the tribunal of heaven. Sweeping a hand over all creation, he pleaded, "Punish me for their mistakes. See the murderer? Give me his penalty. The adulteress? I'll take her shame. The bigot, the liar, the thief? Do to me what you would do to them. Treat me as you would a sinner." And God did.*

   A. Why did innocent Jesus request to take the punishment due to murderers, adulterers, and other sinners?

B. Have you allowed Jesus to take on himself your own sin? Explain.

4. *The path of righteousness is a narrow, winding trail up a steep hill. At the top of the hill is a cross. At the base of the cross are bags. Countless bags full of innumerable sins. Calvary is the compost pile for guilt.*

A. In what way is Calvary "the compost pile for guilt"?

B. If you have set your bag of guilt at the foot of Calvary, describe how this came to be. If you have not already done so, why not?

Traveling Up

1. Read Romans 3:9–18.

A. What does it mean to be "under sin" (NIV)? Who is "under sin" (v. 9)?

B. List the characteristics of being "under sin" (vv. 10–17).

C. How does verse 18 summarize all the characteristics you just listed?

2. Read Isaiah 45:21–25.

A. How does God describe himself in verse 21?

B. What command does God give in verse 22?

C. What prediction does God give in verses 23–24?

D. What promise does God give in verse 25? To whom is he referring?

3. Read Romans 5:6–11 and 1 Peter 3:18.

A. According to Romans 5:6, for whom did Christ die?

B. What drove Christ to die for us (v. 8)?

C. What is the difference between being "justified" and "saved" (v. 9 NIV)?

D. What is the normal response of one who has been "reconciled" (v. 11 NIV)? Is this your response? Explain.

Traveling On

1. Read a contemporary book by an author who exchanged his or her guilt for the forgiveness of God. How does this remind you of your own need for forgiveness?

2. Is there someone in your life whom you need to forgive but haven't? Remember Jesus' words: "But if you do not forgive men their sins, your Father will not forgive your sins" (Matthew 6:15 NIV). Commit today to forgive this person—and if possible, let him or her know what you've done.

9

Get Over Yourself

The Burden of Arrogance

TRAVELING BACK

1. *God . . . doesn't dislike arrogance. He doesn't disapprove of arrogance. He's not unfavorably disposed toward arrogance. God hates arrogance. What a meal of maggots does for our stomach, human pride does for God's.*

   A. Why do you think God dislikes human pride?

   B. Would you consider yourself a prideful person? Would others agree with you? Explain.

2. *God . . . hates arrogance because we haven't done anything to be arrogant about. Do art critics give awards to the canvas? Is there a Pulitzer for ink? Can you imagine a scalpel growing smug after a successful heart transplant? Of course not. They are only tools, so they get no credit for the accomplishments.*

   A. In what way are we "tools" in God's hands?

   B. Is there any room at all for taking pride in one's accomplishments? Explain.

3. *Why does God have anything to do with us? For his name's sake. No other name on the marquee. No other name up in lights. No other name on the front page. This is all done for God's glory.*

   A. Why isn't it vain of God to associate with us for *his* name's sake?

   B. What is meant by "God's glory"? Why is God's glory so important?

4. Consider several ways to cultivate humility and kill ungodly pride:

- Assess yourself honestly.

- Don't take success too seriously.

- Celebrate the significance of others.

- Don't demand your own parking place.

- Never announce your success before it occurs.

- Speak humbly.

- Live at the foot of the cross.

A. Who can help you assess yourself honestly? What does such an assessment reveal?

B. How can you celebrate the significance of others? Who in your immediate circle do you need to celebrate right now?

C. How can you "live at the foot of the cross"? What does this mean?

Traveling Up

1. Read Proverbs 16:5, 18–19.

A. What does the Lord think of the proud (v. 5)? How will he respond to them?

B. What is the outcome of pride (v. 18)?

C. What contrast is made in verse 19? Why is this true?

2. Read Isaiah 57:15–19; 66:2.

A. How does the Lord describe himself in verse 15? With whom is he pleased to live?

B. Why will God not "accuse forever" (v. 16)?

C. How will the Lord respond to those who turn to him in faith (vv. 18–19)?

D. Whom does God esteem, according to Isaiah 66:2? Why does the Lord delight in men and women like this?

3. Read Philippians 2:3–11.

   A. What does verse 3 instruct us not to do? What should we do instead?

   B. What overall instruction do we receive in verse 5?

   C. How did Jesus follow this instruction during his earthly ministry (vv. 6–8)?

   D. How will God reward Jesus for his faithfulness (vv. 9–11)?

   E. In what way are we to emulate Jesus' example? How are you doing in this regard? Explain.

TRAVELING ON

1. Watch a classic movie such as *Citizen Kane* to see how even Hollywood sometimes recognizes the deadly poison of human pride. How does pride ultimately destroy the person who lets it control him or her?

2. Do a Bible study on how God does everything for the sake of his name. Look up references to "the name," "my name," "his name," etc. What do you discover?

10

I Will Lead You Home

The Burden of the Grave

TRAVELING BACK

1. *Someday our Shepherd . . . will take us to the mountain by way of the valley. He will guide us to his house through the valley of the shadow of death.*

   A. Do you think of your own death, or do you avoid the thought? Explain.

   B. Has a believer you were close to ever died? If so, describe how the Shepherd guided him or her through the valley of the shadow of death.

2. *David grants us two important reminders that can help us surrender our fear of the grave. We all have to face it. . . . And though his first reminder sobers us, his second reminder encourages us: We don't have to face death alone.*

   A. If you were to face your own death tomorrow, would you be ready? Explain.

   B. Do you feel as though you would be facing death alone? Explain.

3. *Don't face death without facing God. Don't even speak of death without speaking to God. He and he alone can guide you through the valley. Others may speculate or aspire, but only God knows the way to get you home. And only God is committed to getting you there safely.*

   A. Name a few ways in which God helps his children face death.

   B. How can we be certain God is committed to getting us to heaven safely?

4. *[Jesus] may send missionaries to teach you, angels to protect you, teachers to guide you, singers to inspire you, and physicians to heal you, but he sends no one to take you. He reserves this job for himself.*

   A. When Jesus comes to take you home, what do you think you might say to him first?

   B. Why do you think Jesus insists on coming in person to get you? How does this make you feel?

Traveling Up

1. Read Psalm 116:15; 139:16.

   A. What does Psalm 116:15 say is "precious" to God? Why is this so?

   B. What claim does Psalm 139:16 make? Does this give you comfort? Explain.

2. Read 1 Thessalonians 4:13–18.

   A. What do you learn from this passage about those who die in Christ?

   B. How are these words intended to "encourage" us? Why are we instructed to repeat these words to others?

3. Read 2 Corinthians 5:1–10.

   A. What does Paul mean by "earthly tent" (v. 1 NIV)? Why use this picture?

   B. What is life like in this "tent"? How does Paul contrast life in the "heavenly dwelling" (v.2 NIV)?

   C. What token has God given us to assure us that what he says will one day happen, will actually happen (v. 5)?

   D. How is the information in this passage supposed to make us "confident" (v. 6 NIV)?

   E. What preference does Paul express in verse 8? Why does he prefer this?

   F. How is verse 10 both a promise and a warning?

Traveling On

1. Visit a nearby cemetery, and spend at least an hour reading the gravestones to remind yourself both of death's reality and of the hope believers can have despite its cold embrace.

2. Read Herbert Lockyer's classic book. *Last Words of Saints and Sinners*. How do the deaths of the two groups compare?

11

When Mourning Comes

The Burden of Grief

TRAVELING BACK

1. *The black bag of sorrow is hard to bear. It's hard to bear because not everyone understands your grief. They did at first. They did at the funeral. They did at the graveside. But they don't now; they don't understand. Grief lingers.*

   A. How do you personally deal with sorrow?

   B. How can we help someone whose grief just won't go away?

2. *Only God knows the reasons behind his actions. But here is a key truth on which we can stand. Our God is a good God.*

   A. Why do you think God seldom "explains" his actions in our lives?

   B. How have you personally experienced that God is a good God?

3. *Death is God's way of taking people away from evil. From what kind of evil? An extended disease? An addiction? A dark season of rebellion? We don't know. But we know that no person lives one day more or less than God intends.*

   A. Have you ever thought about death in this way? That it's God's way of taking people away from evil? How do you respond to this idea?

   B. How can the idea of God's sovereignty bring comfort in a time of death? How can the doctrine be used to increase someone's pain?

4. *God will lead you* through, *not around, the valley of the shadow of death. And, by the way, aren't you glad it's just a shadow?*

A. If God really loves us, why doesn't he lead us *around* the valley of the shadow of death? Why lead us *through* it?

B. Is death merely a shadow for you? Explain.

Traveling Up

1. Read Lamentations 3:31–33.

   A. How can verse 31 give you hope when you find yourself engulfed in grief?

   B. What do you learn about God in verse 32?

   C. Why is it important that God does not "willingly" bring us grief (v. 33 NIV)? Why does he bring us grief at all?

2. Read John 16:20–22.

   A. What two promises did Jesus give his disciples in verse 20?

   B. What illustration did Jesus use in verse 21 to picture his promises of verse 20? What can we learn from this illustration?

   C. What promise does Jesus give in verse 22? How certain is this promise? On what is it based? How can it continue to help you today when you face grief?

3. Read 1 Peter 1:3–9.

   A. What great blessing does Peter describe in verses 3–4? Do you share in this blessing? Explain.

   B. What kind of shield are we promised in verse 5?

   C. Does genuine faith exempt one from grief (v. 6)? Why or why not?

   D. How do trials and the grief they bring fit in with the Christian life (v. 7)?

   E. What blessing comes to those who believe in Christ (v. 8)?

   F. What blessing does faith ultimately bring to those who exercise it (v. 9)?

Traveling On

1. Interview someone you know to be gifted in the art of comforting the grieving. Look for someone whom others seek out in a time of loss. Ask the person what he or she does at these times. What do you learn?

2. Do a Bible study on the words *tear* and *tears*. What do you learn?

12

From Panic to Peace

The Burden of Fear

TRAVELING BACK

1. *Jesus flat on the ground? Face in the dirt? Extended hands gripping grass? Body rising and falling with sobs? Face as twisted as the olive trees that surround him? What do we do with this image of Jesus? Simple. We turn to it when we look the same.*

   A. Describe the last time you felt the way Jesus is described above.

   B. How does it help us to know that Jesus felt this way?

2. *When you feel the panic, don't focus on the people; focus on the opening. Good counsel in golf. Good counsel in life. Rather than focus on the fear, focus on the solution.*

   A. What kind of situations make you most fearful?

   B. When you face one of these frightening events, how can you "focus on the opening"? What "solution" can you call upon?

3. *Don't avoid life's Gardens of Gethsemane. Enter them. Just don't enter them alone. And while there, be honest. Pounding the ground is permitted. Tears are allowed. And if you sweat blood, you won't be the first. Do what Jesus did; open your heart.*

   A. How do we try to avoid life's Gardens of Gethsemane? Describe the last time you tried to avoid one.

   B. Is it easy or hard for you to express your emotions like this? Explain.

4. *Don't measure the size of the mountain; talk to the One who can move it. Instead of carrying the world on your shoulders, talk to the One who holds the universe on his. Hope is a look away.*

   A. How do we often try to "measure the size of the mountain"? Why is this a bad idea?

   B. In what way is hope "a look away"? How can prayer help to restore our hope? Does it help restore yours? Explain.

Traveling Up

1. Read Psalm 56:3–4.

   A How does the psalmist deal with his own fears? Do you follow his example? Explain.

   B. Why is the psalmist unafraid of "mortal man" (v. 4 NIV)? Is this a statement of ignorance or something else? Explain.

2. Read Isaiah 41:10–14.

   A. Why does God tell Israel not to fear (v. 10)?

   B. What promise does God give in verses 11–12?

   C. What reason does God give for his promise in verse 13?

   D. What command and promise does God give in verse 14? How can his words encourage you today?

3. Read 1 John 4:16–19.

   A. On what should we rely when we are afraid (v. 16)?

   B. How does John describe God in verse 16? What difference does this make?

   C. How can we have "confidence on the day of judgment" (v. 17 NIV)?

   D. What antidote to fear does John give in verse 18? How does this antidote work?

   E. How is this antidote to be shared? How does this show that we really have the antidote?

Traveling On

1. In your journal write about a time you had "garden" experiences. Explain what situation took you there, how you felt, what prayers you prayed, and how God ministered to you.

2. Read *Foxe's Book of Martyrs* to see how many of God's choicest saints overcame their fear even as they faced death.

13

Silent Nights and Solitary Days

The Burden of Loneliness

TRAVELING BACK

1. *By now you've learned that you don't have to be alone to feel lonely.*

   A. What's the difference between being alone and feeling lonely?

   B. Do you avoid being alone? Explain.

   C. How often, in a normal week, would you say you feel lonely?

2. *Loneliness is not the absence of faces. It is the absence of intimacy. Loneliness doesn't come from being alone; it comes from feeling alone.*

   A. How would you define nonsexual intimacy? With how many friends can you speak intimately? Are you satisfied with this number? Explain.

   B. How do you deal with loneliness? When you feel lonely, what do you do?

3. *Could it be that loneliness is not a curse but a gift? A gift from God? . . . I wonder if loneliness is God's way of getting our attention.*

   A. Do you agree that loneliness can be a gift from God? Explain.

   B. Why might God want to get your attention through loneliness? To what might he want to call your attention?

4. *God changes your* n *into a* v. *You go from lonely to lovely. When you know God loves you, you won't be desperate for the love of others.*

   A. How does assurance of God's love for you, personally, change everything?

   B. Does knowledge of God's love eliminate the need for intimate friends? Explain.

C. What's the difference between desiring the love of others and being desperate for it?

TRAVELING UP

1. Read Psalm 88.

   A. How would you describe the man who wrote this psalm?

   B. Why do you think God included this psalm in the Bible?

   C. Have you ever felt as the psalmist did in verses 13–14? Explain.

   D. Most psalms do not end as this one does (v. 18). Why do you think it ends like this? Is this a comfort to you? Explain.

2. Read Deuteronomy 31:6–8.

   A. What command does God give the Israelites in verse 6? What encouragement does he give them?

   B. Why do you suppose that Moses repeats to Joshua both the command and the encouragement in verses 7–8? What does this suggest to you about dealing with your own fears?

3. Read John 14:16–18; Matthew 28:16–20.

   A. What request did Jesus say he would make of the Father in John 14:16?

   B. What promise did Jesus make in John 14:18? How is he fulfilling this promise today?

   C. How can we take courage from Jesus' words in Matthew 28:18?

   D. What encouragement can we get from Jesus' final words in Matthew 28:20? Are you relying on this promise? Why or why not?

TRAVELING ON

1. Examine your schedule, and find an entire day when you can plan to get alone, just you and God. Go to a retreat center, a solitary spot, a place in the woods, any place where you can spend a whole

day in solitude. Bring your Bible, and make no other plans than to spend the day alone with God.

2. Get a group of your believing friends together, and spend a few hours visiting some of your church's shut-ins, whether at their homes or in care centers. Relieve their loneliness for a while.

14

The Crowing Rooster and Me

The Burden of Shame

TRAVELING BACK

1. *Is Peter the only person to do the very thing he swore he'd never do? "Infidelity is behind me!" "From now on, I'm going to bridle my tongue." "No more shady deals. I've learned my lesson." Oh, the volume of our boasting. And, oh, the heartbreak of our shame.*

    A. Describe a time when you followed Peter's example and did the very thing you swore you'd never do. What happened?

    B. Why do you think we engage in such foolish boasting? What do we think we'll gain?

2. *We weep as Peter wept, and we do what Peter did. We go fishing. We go back to our old lives. We return to our pre-Jesus practices. We do what comes naturally, rather than what comes spiritually. And we question whether Jesus has a place for folks like us.*

    A. Have you ever "gone fishing" or returned to your pre-Jesus practices after a spiritual failure? If so, how did you feel at the time?

    B. Why do we question whether Jesus has a place for folks like us? Have you ever felt this way? Explain.

3. *Jesus prepared a table in the presence of the enemy. Judas was allowed to see the supper, but he wasn't allowed to stay there. You are not welcome here. This table is for my children. You may tempt them. You may trip them. But you will never sit with them. This is how much he loves us.*

A. Why do you think Jesus allowed Judas to see the supper? Why not banish him before the disciples gathered?

B. What does the Lord's Supper mean to you personally? What goes through your mind during the service?

4. *The same Jesus who'd prepared a meal for Peter had prepared one for me. The same Shepherd who had trumped the devil trumped him again. The same Savior who had built a fire on the shore stirred a few embers in my heart. "Every one of you drink this." And so I did. It felt good to be back at the table.*

A. Why do you think Jesus prepared a meal for Peter, who denied him, but not for Judas, who betrayed him? What was the difference?

B. How do the stories of both Peter and Max show true repentance? How does Jesus always respond to true repentance? Why is this important to understand?

TRAVELING UP

1. Read Joel 2:25–27.

A. What promise does God make to his people who repent (v. 25)?

B. Why do you think God twice says in verses 26–27 that his people will never again be shamed? Why does God care about getting rid of shame?

2. Read 2 Timothy 2:15–16.

A. What instruction is given in verse 15? How can you comply with this command?

B. How can we avoid being ashamed, according to verse 15?

C. How does verse 16 continue to tell us how to avoid being ashamed?

3. Read Hebrews 12:2–3.

A. What are we instructed to do in verse 2? How can this keep us from being ashamed?

B. How did Jesus react to the shame of the cross? Why was there shame at the cross?

C. How are we to benefit from the example of Jesus on the cross?

TRAVELING ON

1. Think of Max's story and how shame kept him from fellowship with God. Be honest with yourself, and ask if you're dealing with anything similar. If so, follow Max's courageous example, and admit this "shameful thing" to a trusted and godly friend. Break its power over you by confessing and forsaking it—and be glad at the Lord's table once more.

2. If you ever have the opportunity, attend a Seder prepared by someone who can explain the Messianic significance of this ancient Jewish meal. Enrich your appreciation of the Lord's Supper.

15

Slippery Sheep and Healed Hurts

The Burden of Disappointment

TRAVELING BACK

1. *A disappointment is a missed appointment. What we hoped would happen, didn't. We wanted health; we got disease. We wanted retirement; we got reassignment. Divorce instead of family. Dismissal instead of promotion.*

   A. What disappointments have you had to face recently?

   B. What do you do with your disappointments?

2. *Just like sheep, we have wounds, but ours are wounds of the heart that come from disappointment after disappointment. If we're not careful, these wounds lead to bitterness. And so just like sheep, we need to be treated.*

   A. How do repeated disappointments lead to bitterness?

   B. What kinds of things have made you bitter? How do you deal with bitterness?

3. *The large portion of our problems are not lion-sized attacks, but rather the day-to-day swarm of frustrations and mishaps and heartaches.*

   A. What little things in life tend to frustrate you the most?

   B. What help can you offer to someone plagued with a swarm of mishaps or heartaches?

4. *Jesus tends to his sheep. And he will tend to you. If you will let him. How? How do you let him? The steps are so simple. First, go to him. Second, assume the right posture. Bow before God. Third, trust in him.*

   A. How can you "go to" Jesus? What does it mean to "go to" him?

   B. Why is it necessary to "bow" before God? What does this mean?

C. What does it mean to "trust" in God? How do we do this, practically speaking?

TRAVELING UP

1. Read Psalm 22:2–5.

    A. What disappointment did David suffer in verse 2? Have you ever felt like this? Explain.

    B. How did David combat his disappointment in verses 3–5?

    C. What was the result of the ancestors' trust described in verses 4–5? How is this meant to encourage us?

    D. Consider that this is the psalm Jesus quoted while hanging on the cross. What do you think the psalm taught him about disappointment?

2. Read Romans 5:1–5.

    A. How do we gain peace with God (v. 1)?

    B. What benefit does this peace gain us (v. 2)? How should this make us feel?

    C. What relationship does sufferings have to hope (vv. 3–5)?

    D. Why does hope not disappoint us (v. 5)? How does this matter to us on a day-to-day level?

3. Read Psalm 147:1–3.

    A. How did the Israelites deal with their disappointments (v. 1)?

    B. What encouragement does God give his people in verse 3?

    C. How do you think God heals the brokenhearted? What has he done in your own life?

TRAVELING ON

1. Make a list of your biggest disappointments in life. Write them down. Then take each one, in order, to God in prayer. Give them to him explicitly, one by one.

2. Make a new commitment to get involved in regular prayer. Set a time. Set a place. Set a specific period. Prepare a list of concerns and thanks to bring to God. Then do it.

16

Jam Session

The Burden of Envy

TRAVELING BACK

1. *Jealousy sets her cross hairs on the one who has more.*

    A. Describe a time when you felt jealous of someone. What prompted your jealousy?

    B. Why do most of us want "more"? What keeps us from being content with what we have?

2. *If focusing on our diminishing items leads to envy, what would happen if we focused on the unending items? If awareness of what we don't have creates jealousy, is it possible that an awareness of our abundance will lead to contentment?*

    A. Answer both of the preceding questions.

    B. Try to itemize the "unending items" that you possess. What's on your list?

    C. Try to list your "abundance." What does this tell you about God's provision?

3. *God is not a miser with his grace. Your cup may be low on cash or clout, but it is overflowing with mercy. You may not have the prime parking place, but you have sufficient pardon.*

    A. How often do you ponder God's grace to you? His mercy?

    B. How has God been gracious to you this week? This month? This year?

4. *One thing is certain. When the final storm comes and you are safe in your Father's house, you won't regret what he didn't give. You'll be stunned at what he did.*

A. Try to imagine the day you arrive safe in your Father's house. Look around. What has he given you?

B. How can meditating on your eternal future with God help you to deal with what exists today?

TRAVELING UP

1. Read Proverbs 14:30; 23:17.

   A. With what does Proverbs 14:30 contrast envy? How is this significant?

   B. In what ways do believers sometimes envy "sinners" (Prov. 23:17)?

   C. What does it mean to be "zealous for the fear of the LORD" (NIV)?

2. Read James 3:13–4:5.

   A. What in verse 13 does James contrast with "bitter envy" in verse 14?

   B. Where does envy come from (v. 15)?

   C. What always accompanies envy (v. 16)?

   D. What causes fights and quarrels among spiritual brothers (4:1)?

   F. God himself is said to "envy" in 4:5 (NIV). How does this differ from human envy?

3. Read Titus 3:3–7.

   A. How does Paul describe his pre-Christian life (v. 3)? What do you think he envied?

   B. How did God deliver us from envy (vv. 4–5)?

   C. To what extent did God pour out his Holy Spirit on us (v. 6)? How is this meant to nip envy in the bud?

   D. What was the purpose of God's saving us (v. 7)? How can meditating on this truth destroy envy?

Traveling On

1. Draw a line down a sheet of paper, creating two columns. On the left side, list some of the things you envy in others. On the right side, list what God has supplied you in abundance and, if possible, include a Scripture reference. For example, in the left column you might say "I wish I had better health," and beside it, in the right column, you might list "God will give me a glorious, eternal body (Phil. 3:20–21)."

2. Make a date to serve dinner at a local rescue mission or homeless shelter. Try not to schedule your visit at Thanksgiving or Christmas (since such service organizations usually have more than enough help during those two holidays). And be thankful for what God has given you.

17

God's Loving Pursuit

The Burden of Doubt

TRAVELING BACK

1. *When Jesus found us, we acted like Eric. Our limitations kept us from recognizing the One who came to save us. We even doubted his presence—and sometimes we still do.*

    A. Do you ever doubt God's presence? If so, why?

    B. How do our limitations keep us from recognizing the One who came to save us? How can we overcome these limitations?

2. *If the Lord is the shepherd who leads the flock, goodness and mercy are the two sheepdogs who guard the rear of the flock.*

    A. How does "goodness" differ from "mercy"? How are they the same?

    B. Where in your life do you most need God's goodness and mercy right now? Why don't you take the time to talk to him about your need?

3. *Trust your faith and not your feelings. . . . Measure your value through God's eyes, not your own. . . . See the big picture, not the small.*

    A. How do we sometimes trust our feelings and not our faith? How can we stop making this mistake?

    B. Take a few minutes to describe your value in God's eyes. What has he said about you in the Bible?

    C. How can we see the big picture, not the small?

4. *Most of all, God gives us himself. Even when we choose our hovel over his house and our trash over his grace, still he follows. Never forcing us.*

Never leaving us. Patiently persistent. Faithfully present. Using all of his power to convince us that he is who he is and that he can be trusted to lead us home.

A. How do you know God has given you himself? How can you be sure of this?

B. How has God used his power to convince you he is who he is? What most convinces you that God can be trusted to lead you home?

Traveling Up

1. Read James 1:5–8.

A. To whom is verse 5 addressed? Do you qualify? Explain.

B. What promise does verse 5 make?

C. What condition is placed in verse 6 on the promise of verse 5?

D. To what does James compare someone who doubts God's promise? Why is this picture appropriate?

E. What warning is given in verses 7 and 8? In what way are these individuals "double-minded" (NIV)? How can one correct such a serious problem?

2. Read Jude 20–22.

A. What instruction is given in verse 20? How is this instruction to be carried out?

B. What instruction is given in verse 21? What future event empowers us to follow this instruction?

C. What instruction is given in verse 22? Why do you think the command was given? How can we comply with this command?

3. Read Romans 14:19–23.

A. Describe the command in verse 19. What is the purpose of this command? How well do you fulfill it? Explain.

B. How is it possible to destroy someone for the sake of food (v. 20)?

C. How does verse 21 relate to doubt?

D. What command is given in verse 22? What blessing is available? What does this blessing mean?

E. How is verse 23 an effective guideline for the entire Christian life? What rule is laid out here?

TRAVELING ON

1. Realize that there is a great difference between doubt and questions. Doubt disbelieves in the promises and good character of God; questions merely wonder how God might pull off some incredible feat. To get a "feel" for the difference between doubt and questions, study the vastly different ways God responded to Zechariah in Luke 1:5–20 and Mary in Luke 1:26–38. They asked similar questions ("How can I be sure of this?" versus "How will this be?" [NIV]) regarding miraculous pregnancies, but one was judged and the other blessed. Why?

2. Read Os Guinness's book *God in the Dark* for a clear and helpful discussion on doubt.

18

Almost Heaven

The Burden of Homesickness

TRAVELING BACK

1. *The twists and turns of life have a way of reminding us—we aren't home here. This is not our homeland. We aren't fluent in the languages of disease and death. The culture confuses the heart, the noise disrupts our sleep, and we feel far from home. And, you know what? That's OK.*

   A. Why do we often forget that this is not our real home?

   B. In what ways do you feel like a foreigner on this earth? Are you OK with that? Explain.

2. *Homesickness is one of the burdens God doesn't mind if we carry. We . . . are being prepared for another house. And we . . . know we aren't there yet.*

   A. Do you feel "homesick" for heaven? Explain.

   B. How is God preparing you for "another house"?

3. *The greatest calamity is not to feel far from home when you are, but to feel right at home when you are not.*

   A. Could it be that much of the disappointment we feel in life comes from trying to feel right at home when we're not? Explain.

   B. How can we consciously guard against feeling at home in this world? Name several practical things we can do.

4. *Every wrinkle and every needle take us one step closer to the last step when Jesus will change our simple bodies into forever bodies. No pain. No depression. No sickness. No end.*

   A. How does your own body remind you that this is not your forever home?

B. How would you respond to someone who says this desire for an eternal, painless body is merely wishful thinking and you'd be better off getting all the gusto while you can?

TRAVELING UP

1. Read Philippians 1:20–23.

   A. Describe Paul's firm expectation in verse 20. What challenge faced him?

   B. In your own words, explain what Paul meant in verse 21.

   C. Describe Paul's dilemma in verse 22. Why was he so torn?

   D. What did Paul mean by "depart" in verse 23 (NIV)? Depart where? Why would this be "better"?

2. Read Philippians 3:17–4:1.

   A. How does Paul describe the enemies of Christ in verses 18–19? What traits characterize them?

   B. Describe the main contrast of these people with believers in Christ (v. 20).

   C. For whom are Christians waiting (vv. 20–21)? What are they waiting for him to do?

   D. What effect should meditating on this truth have on believers (4:1)? Does it have this effect on you? Explain.

3. Read 1 Corinthians 15:50–57.

   A. What two contrasts does Paul make in verse 50? Why should this matter to us? Why is it important?

   B. What "secret" or "mystery" does Paul describe in verses 51–52?

   C. What kind of "clothes" will believers wear in heaven (v. 53)? Why is this important?

   D. Restate the message of verses 54–57 in your own words. Imagine that you are describing this situation to an eight-year-old.

   E. Are you "homesick"? Why or why not?

Traveling On

1. Do a study in the four Gospels and in the Book of Acts on the Lord Jesus' postresurrection body. Describe it. Then realize that our resurrection bodies will look and act similar to his!

2. Read Joni Eareckson Tada's book titled *Heaven*. Joni has lived in a wheelchair for decades since a diving accident at age seventeen, so she expresses a uniquely powerful vision of heaven.

Hope. Pure and simple.

The Teaching Ministry of Max Lucado

You're invited to partner with UpWords to bring radio and the Internet a message of hope, pure and simple, in Jesus Christ!

Visit www.maxlucado.com to find FREE valuable resources for spiritual growth and encouragement, such as:

- Archives of UpWords, Max's daily radio program. You will also find a listing of radio stations and broadcast times in your area.

- Daily devotionals

- Book excerpts

- Exclusive features and presentations

- Subscription information on how you can receive email messages from Max

- Downloads of audio, video, and printed material

You will also find an online store and special offers.

Call toll-free,
1-800-822-9673

for more information and to order by phone.

UpWords Ministries
P.O. Box 692170
San Antonio, TX 78269-2170
1-800-822-9673
www.maxlucado.com

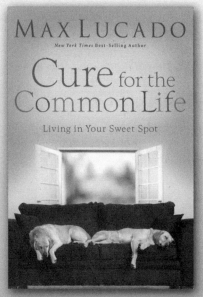

Other *Cure for the Common Life* Products

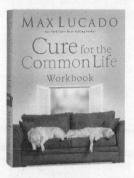

In the *Cure for the Common Life Workbook*, Max teaches that you are a unique individual, created in God's image, with your own gifts, strengths, and passions. In this exciting companion to the trade book, Max provides practical tools and assessments for exploring and identifying your own uniqueness. He motivates you to put your uniqueness into practice and gives you perspective to redefine "work."

It's never too late to discover your strengths, God's will for your life, or to redirect your career—and cure the otherwise hopeless prognosis of a common life.

Cure for the Common Life Webinar

Visit www.maxlucado.com/discoverthecure to hear directly from Max about *Cure for the Common Life* and to access a helpful tool that takes you on a journey to discover your S.T.O.R.Y.

Listen to the message of *Cure for the Common Life* in your home or take it on the road. This CD makes the perfect gift for the family or friends you know are struggling to find their "sweet spot."

Cure for the Common Life is also available in Spanish

GRUPO NELSON
Desde 1798

Para otros materiales, visítenos a:
gruponelson.com

AN ANGEL'S STORY

Was the birth of Jesus a quietly profound event? Or could it have included heavenly battles, angel armies, and a scheming Satan? Come along as Lucado takes us on a journey into his imagination—pulling back the curtain as we see what might have taken place in *An Angel's Story* (previously titled *Cosmic Christmas*).

AND THE ANGELS WERE SILENT

As Jesus entered His final days and faced Golgotha, He acted with loving purpose and deliberate intent. Each step was calculated. Every act premeditated. *And the Angels Were Silent* allows you to enter and observe a revealing and intimate view of our Savior's last week.

Spanish edition available

THE APPLAUSE OF HEAVEN

It is what you always dreamed but never expected. It's having God as your dad, your biggest fan, and your best friend. It is having the King of Kings in your cheering section. It is hearing the applause of heaven. Max Lucado believes that the Beatitudes provide what we need to discover the joy of God. Much more than a how-to book on happiness, *The Applause of Heaven* is an encounter with the Source of Joy.

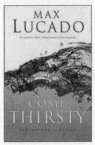

Large Print and Spanish editions available

COME THIRSTY

Scientists assure us we can't live without water. But survival without God? We sip, we taste, but we often go without a drink from the Lord's well. And we pay the price. We shrink and hearts harden. This life-giving book leads us to the four nutrients needed by every soul. Come to the cross and know your sins are pardoned and your death is defeated. Receive Christ's energy and believe you can do all things through the One who gives you strength. Receive his Lordship, knowing you belong to Him and that He looks out for you. Receive His love and feel confident nothing can separate you from it.

For an audio/visual presentation and to learn more about *Come Thirsty*, visit www.maxlucado.com/come.thirsty

THE CHRISTMAS CHILD

A Chicago journalist finds himself in a small Texas town on Christmas eve. Lonely and alone, he encounters old faces and new facts . . . a handcarved manger, a father's guilt, a young girl's faith. The trip into the past holds his key to the future, and a scarlet cross shows him the way home.

A GENTLE THUNDER

How far do you want God to go in getting your attention? Don't answer too quickly. What if God moved you to another land? (As He did Abraham.) What if He called you out of retirement? (Remember Moses?) How about the voice of an angel or the bowel of a fish (Gideon and Jonah.) God does what it takes to get our attention. That's the message of this book: the relentless pursuit of God.

Spanish edition available

GIVE IT ALL TO HIM

In this story a woman gives her garbage of shame to the trash man; an old man hands over his heavy bag of regrets. Hundreds walk to the landfill and find it filled with trash.

"You can't live with this," he explains. "You weren't made to."

For individuals and churches, here is a beautiful story of a Savior who can take all our garbage on his shoulders—and amazingly, still stand!

In addition to this story, Max explains in easy-to-understand language what Christ did for us and how to turn in our old baggage and exchange it for new life in him.

For a moving audio/visual presentation of *Give It All to Him,* visit www.maxlucado.com/give.it.all.

THE GREAT HOUSE OF GOD

Using the Lord's Prayer as a floor plan for *The Great House of God,* Max Lucado introduces us to a God who desires his children to draw close to him. Warm your heart by the fire in the living room. Nourish your spirit in the kitchen. Step into the hallway and find forgiveness. No house is more complete, no foundation more solid. So come to the house built just for you, *The Great House of God.*

Spanish edition available

HE CHOSE THE NAILS

Christ's sacrifice has defined the very essence of mankind's faith for the past 2000 years. Now Max Lucado invites you to examine the cross, contemplate its purpose, and celebrate its significance. With his warm, caring style, Max examines the symbols surrounding Christ's crucifixion, revealing the claims of the cross and asserting that if they are true, then Christianity itself is true. The supporting evidence either makes the cross the single biggest hoax of all time, or the hope of all humanity.

Large Print and Spanish editions available

HE DID THIS JUST FOR YOU

Spanish edition available

Building on stories and illustrations from the book *He Chose the Nails* by Max Lucado, *He Did This Just for You* is a 64-page evangelistic book that leads the readers through God's plan of salvation and offers an invitation to accept Christ. It's the perfect way to introduce the gospel to friends and acquaintances through Max Lucado's warm and easy to understand writing style. Experience God's grace and plan of salvation for the first time or use this booklet to share the message of hope with someone you know.

HE STILL MOVES STONES

Why does the Bible contain so many stories of hurting people? Though their situations vary, their conditions don't. They have nowhere to turn. Yet before their eyes stands a never-say-die Galilean who majors in stepping in when everyone else steps out. Lucado reminds us that the purpose of these portraits isn't to tell us what Jesus *did*—but rather to remind us what Jesus still *does*.

Spanish edition available

A HEART LIKE JESUS

The heart of Jesus is sacred, and the lessons and examples it provides to us are paramount in our daily mission to follow in His footsteps. Max Lucado poses the question "what if, for one day and night, your heart was replaced by the heart of Christ?" That thought-provoking question leads to many personal revelations demonstrating that we can recast our hearts to be more like that of Jesus.

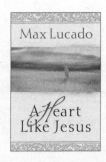

In the Eye of the Storm

Come face-to-face with Jesus when He experienced more stress than any other day of his life aside from his crucifixion. Before the morning became evening, he has reason to weep, run, shout, curse, praise, and doubt. If you know what it means to be caught in life's storms . . . if you've ever ridden the roller coaster of sorrow and celebration . . . if you've ever wondered if God in heaven can relate to you on earth, then this book will encourage and inspire you.

Spanish edition available

In the Grip of Grace

Large Print and Spanish editions available

Can anything separate us from the love of God? Can you drift too far? Wait too long? Out-sin the love of God? The answer is found in one of life's sweetest words—grace. Max Lucado shows how you can't fall beyond God's love. "God doesn't condone our sin, nor does He compromise His standard. Rather than dismiss our sin, He assumes our sin and incredibly, sentences Himself. God is still holy. Sin is still sin. And we are redeemed."

Just For You

This artistic, full-color book will speak to your heart by combining the incredible images of The Visual Bible movies with the dynamic text of Lucado's classic book, *He Chose the Nails*. Prepare to experience the unmistakable power of the cross as you see how and why Jesus chose to undergo the ultimate sacrifice . . . just for you.

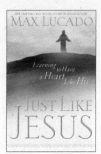

JUST LIKE JESUS

"What if, for one day, Jesus became you?" asks master storyteller Max Lucado. With this simple premise, Lucado tells how God loves you just the way you are, but He refuses to leave you there. He wants you to have a heart like His. He wants you to be just like Jesus.

Large Print and Spanish editions available

JUST LIKE JESUS DEVOTIONAL

This personal month-long journey with the Savior offers Scripture, practical devotions and application sessions to pattern one's life after Christ. Starting at day one, readers meet the Savior and find their way of thinking challenged. As readers begin to think more like Christ, they are challenged to put words into action as the journey escalates into a full force, radical retracing and renewal of what it means to be a follower of Christ.

A LOVE WORTH GIVING

Finding it hard to love? Someone in your world is hard to forgive? Is patience an endangered species? Kindness a forgotten virtue? If so, you may have forgotten an essential first step. Living loved. God loves you. Personally. Powerfully. Passionately. Others have promised and failed. But God has promised and succeeded. He loves you with an unfailing love. And his love—if you let it—can fill you and leave you with a love worth giving.

Spanish edition available

Next Door Savior

The universe's Commander in Chief knows your name. He has walked your streets. Endowed with sleepless attention and endless devotion, He listens. The fact that we can't imagine how He hears a million requests as if they were only one doesn't mean He can't or doesn't. For He can and does. There is no person He won't touch. No place He won't go to find you. For even though He is in heaven, He never left the neighborhood. He is near enough to touch. Strong enough to trust. A next-door Savior.

Hear all about *Next Door Savior* from Max himself at http://www.maxlucado.com/nds.

Large Print and Spanish editions available

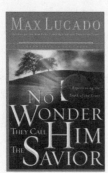

No Wonder They Call Him Savior

In this compelling quest for the Messiah, best-selling author Max Lucado invites readers to meet the blue-collar Jew whose claim altered a world and whose promise has never been equaled. Readers will come to know Jesus the Christ in a brand-new way as Lucado brings them full circle to the foot of the cross and the man who sacrificed His life on it.

Traveling Light Journal

Dare to slow down, take a break from the chaos of life and commit to meeting Christ like you never thought possible. Find yourself on a 30-day journey, led by Max Lucado, to better understand Psalm 23 and its power to teach you how to lighten your load. Each day includes a Scripture verse, a devotional excerpt, a short prayer, and space to write thoughts and prayers.

When Christ Comes

Thoughts of the Second Coming are unsettling. Open graves and occupied clouds. Sins revealed and evil unveiled. Yet, for Max Lucado, the coming of Christ will be "the beginning of the very best." In *When Christ Comes*, Lucado shares how Christians can live in hope, confident in his comfort and peaceful in our preparations for His return.

Spanish edition available

When God Whispers Your Name

Do you find it hard to believe that the One who made everything keeps your name on His heart and on His lips? Did you realize that your name is written on the hand of God (Isa. 49:16)? Perhaps you've never seen your name honored. And you can't remember when you heard it spoken with kindness. In this book, Lucado offers the inspiration to believe that God has already bought the ticket with your name on it.

Large Print and Spanish editions available

THE CAMPAIGN TO MAKE
POVERTY HISTORY
WWW.ONE.ORG

There is a plague of biblical proportions taking place in Africa right now, but we can beat this crisis, if we each do our part. Step ONE is signing the ONE petition, to join the ONE Campaign.

The ONE Campaign is a new effort to rally Americans—ONE by ONE—to fight global AIDS and extreme poverty. We are engaging Americans everywhere we gather—in churches and synagogues, on the internet and college campuses, at community meetings and concerts. To learn more about The ONE Campaign, go to www.one.org and sign the online petition.

"Use your uniqueness to take great risks for God! If you're great with kids, volunteer at the orphanage. If you have a head for business, start a soup kitchen. If God bent you toward medicine, dedicate a day or a decade to AIDS patients. The only mistake is not to risk making one."

—Max Lucado, *Cure for the Common Life*

ONE Voice can make a difference.
Let God work through you; join the ONE Campaign now!

This campaign is brought to you by